The making of
SCARFACE

ALSO AVAILABLE IN THIS SERIES:

The Making of *Taxi Driver*
The Making of *Raging Bull*
The Making of *The Great Rock and Roll Swindle*

The making of
SCARFACE

DAVID TAYLOR

The publisher wishes to thank the Book Division at Lasgo Chrysalis London for their ongoing support in developing this series.

Published by Unanimous Ltd.
Unanimous Ltd. is an imprint of MQ Publications Ltd.
12 The Ivories, 6–8 Northampton Street, London, N1 2HY
Tel: 44 (0)20 7359 2244 Fax: 44 (0)20 7359 1616
email: mail@mqpublications.com
website: www.mqpublications.com

Printed and bound in France

ISBN: 1 90331 873 4

1 2 3 4 5 6 7 8 9

contents

Fade in...   7
Part One: the first cut is the deepest   13
Part Two: cutting edge   55
Part Three: the final cut   173
Fade out...   207
Appendices   211
Selected bibliography   225
Index   227
Acknowledgments   232

fade in...

> "I want what's coming to me…
> The world, chico, and everything in it."
>
> *Tony Montana*

It began, like so many artistic flights of fancy, with a sleepless night. The year was 1980.

"I was watching the old Paul Muni version of *Scarface* about three o'clock in the morning when I couldn't sleep," recounts film producer Martin Bregman. "It occurred to me that a film like *Scarface*—the rise and fall of an American gangster—had not been done recently."

Bregman, a gravel-voiced New Yorker who bears a remarkable resemblance to the actor Chazz Palminteri (Palminteri is best known for playing Cheech, the literary-minded mobster in *Bullets Over Broadway* and Dave Kujan, the customs officer quizzing Kevin Spacey in *The Usual Suspects*), was born in 1931, a year before *Scarface* had been released. He had begun his career as a Hollywood agent and personal manager, helping mould the careers of talents such as Alan Alda, Liza Minnelli, Barbra Streisand, and Candice Bergen. He had also taken a young actor named Al Pacino under his wing when the latter was first embarking on a film career, suggesting he try out for the lead role in a film entitled *Panic in Needle Park* (1971). Just a few months later, Bregman was pushing the virtually unknown Pacino into fighting to play Michael Corleone in *The Godfather* (1972), despite the fact that the studio wanted a big-name star such as Warren Beatty or Robert Redford in the role.

Since those days, Bregman and Pacino had become close personal friends. When Bregman had decided to branch out into producing movies, his first project was *Serpico* in 1973, with Pacino playing the idealistic cop exposing corruption in the police force. They had followed this popular and critical success by collaborating on *Dog Day Afternoon* in 1975, with Pacino as a young bisexual bank robber. Those two films— and the eight Academy Award nominations they had garnered between them—not only helped to consolidate Pacino's reputation as one of the most magnetic and versatile performers of his generation, but also established Bregman as a force to be reckoned with in Hollywood.

The gangster movie had actually enjoyed a resurgence of popularity in the early 1970s. This was partly as a result of the runaway success of *The Godfather*, which Francis Ford Coppola had freely adapted from the bestselling novel by Mario Puzo and transformed into a somber study of power, politics, and family. Since then, a number of film-makers had jumped onto the bandwagon with fanciful biopics of America's most notorious outlaws—*Dillinger* (1973), *Lucky Luciano* (1974), *Lepke* (1975), and *Capone* (1975)—as well as any number of cheap, sexy, violent B-movies that had no ambitions beyond turning a quick buck at the box office.

What Bregman had in mind, however, was something altogether more elaborate. "A gangster opera" was how he described it: a big-budget gangster movie of the old school, tailored for the more sophisticated modern moviegoer. "My concept was to do a film about the rise and fall of an

American gangster—or, rather, an American businessman. Because that was what the original *Scarface* was."

He thought it would be the perfect vehicle for Pacino, who had yet to play a full-throttle villainous role in the movies. "I talked to Al about *Scarface*. I said 'There's something here. But I don't know where it is yet'."

"I had heard a lot about *Scarface* but had never seen it," Pacino admitted.

A few years previously, in 1975, the actor had been appearing in a stage production of *The Resistible Rise of Arturo Ui* by Bertolt Brecht. Written in 1941 as a satire about the rise of National Socialism in Germany, this blackly comical tale revolved around a ruthless mobster attempting to muscle in on the Chicago grocery trade. In writing the play, Brecht had been heavily influenced by *Scarface* and other famous gangster films of the 1930s.

At the time Pacino was starring in *Arturo Ui*, it was almost impossible to screen *Scarface* in the United States. The film's producer, Howard Hughes, had grown increasingly eccentric and unpredictable during the last few years of his life and had attempted to round up all copies of the movie to take it out of circulation. The only thing that had stopped him from getting hold of the original negative was that it was in the possession of the film's director, Howard Hawks, who refused to give it to him. As a result, the only way to see *Scarface* was either in Europe, where a few prints had slipped through the net, or by tracking down a bootleg copy. It wasn't until the end of the 1970s, several years after Hughes's death, that his Sunna Corporation sold on the rights to the film to Universal Pictures and it became freely available again.

Not long after Bregman had broached the subject of a *Scarface* remake, Pacino chanced upon a screening of the movie. "I was walking one day along Sunset Boulevard, of all places, and there was the Tiffany Theater and *Scarface* was playing on a double bill. There were a few of us, so I said 'Why don't we go and take a look at it?' So we went in and it was an astounding movie. The performance of Paul Muni was inspiring. And I just thought, after that, that I just wanted to imitate him. I was inspired by that performance.

"I called Marty Bregman and he started working on developing it as a film."

Scarface was ready to be reborn.

part one:

the first cut
is the deepest

1

"Where'd you get the beauty scar, tough guy?
Eatin' pussy?"

Immigration Officer

The legend was born in 1917 in a Coney Island bar called the Harvard Inn.

On that fateful evening, a New York mobster named Frank Gallucio was enjoying a drink with two lady companions. One of the waiters at the bar began making eyes and flirting with one of the women. She was on the verge of politely asking him to stop pestering her, when the cocky 18-year-old leaned over and confided to her "Honey, you have a nice ass and I mean that as a compliment."

Unfortunately, the woman to whom the waiter had delivered this rather salacious observation was Gallucio's younger sister, Lena. Infuriated, the mobster turned on the young punk, whipping a flick knife from his pocket and viciously slashing him three times across the left side of his face. It has never been established whether Gallucio was actually aiming for his neck.

The waiter's name was Alphonse Capone and the incident left him with 30 stitches in his face and a lifelong reminder of his impertinence.

It also earned him a new nickname.

Scarface.

In later years, Al Capone was to bogusly claim that he had

been left with the scars as a result of fighting in France during World War One. He was extraordinarily sensitive about his disfigurement, carefully powdering his face each morning in an effort to disguise the livid scar tissue. For the rest of his life, he always insisted on presenting the unmarked right side of his face to be photographed. There were few people who were either brave or foolish enough to refer to Capone as Scarface in his presence.

Al Capone was born in Brooklyn in 1899, the fourth son of a tightly knit family of Italian immigrants. His father was a barber and his mother a seamstress, and there is nothing in Al's early youth to suggest that he would rise to become America's most notorious gang leader. He came from a loving home and was, by all accounts, a quiet and studious child.

All that changed when Al reached his early teens. He was expelled from school at the age of 14 after he was hit by one of his teachers and responded in kind. By then he had already begun hanging out with various local street gangs, including the South Brooklyn Rippers and Five Points Youths. He had also found a surrogate father-figure in Johnny Torrio, a local Brooklyn gangster, and had begun running errands for him.

Torrio was the epitome of the gentleman gangster. He impressed upon the young Capone the importance of creating a strict demarcation line between his domestic life and his "professional" career. At home, Torrio was the consummate family man and a highly respected community leader. To the New York underworld, he masterminded a wide network of criminal enterprises, involving prostitution, gambling and protection rackets.

Al listened and learned.

Johnny Torrio later left Brooklyn and relocated to Chicago, then one of the industrial hearts of America and the center of the country's meatpacking industry. Chicago had grown out of a small prairie town surrounded by swampland and, by the turn of the century, was already the second largest city in the United States, a grim metropolis where the air hung heavy with smoke from the nearby factories and the gutters ran with blood from the local abattoirs. It seems hardly surprising that this dank, polluted labyrinth served as the killing ground of America's first recorded serial killer, a charming monster who went by the name of Henry Holmes and who lured unsuspecting women back to his converted townhouse, in which he had installed his own private torture dungeon and cremation chamber.

There were several fortunes to be made in Chicago by any criminal entrepreneur willing to provide suitable leisure activities for the city's blue-collar workforce, not to mention the numerous opportunities available for setting up protection rackets and for muscling in on the various trade unions.

After Torrio's departure from New York, Capone came under the influence of another local mentor: an immigrant from Calabria in southern Italy called Francesco Ioele, but better known locally as Frankie Yale. Ioele was the complete antithesis of the businesslike Johnny Torrio, a brutal mobster who ran his criminal enterprises through fear and intimidation. He liked the young Capone and had given him the job at the Harvard Inn. But after the incident involving Frank and Lena Gallucio, Ioele and his fellow mobster Charles "Lucky" Luciano compelled Capone to make a humiliating public apology to Gallucio in order to teach him respect.

Al listened and learned.

In 1918, it almost looked as if Al Capone had outgrown his youthful transgressions and was about to embark on a legitimate career. He had married a pretty Irish girl from his neighborhood, Mae Coughlin, and they had a son. Al moved his family to Baltimore, where he found a job as a book-keeper for a local construction firm.

Then, in 1921, the Capone family abruptly upped and relocated to Chicago. Al was reunited with Johnny Torrio, who invited him to join his fast-expanding underworld empire and help create order out of chaos, to begin laying the foundations of what would later become referred to as "organized crime". Prohibition was already in full swing throughout the United States. The Volstead Act had come into effect in January 1920 and implemented the 18th Amendment to the US Constitution, which outlawed the manufacture, sale, transportation and importation of alcoholic beverages. Bootlegging and speakeasies were now big business in Chicago. Al became Torrio's partner in crime and later assumed full control of the business when the elder mobster decided to retire to Italy.

Capone was feared and respected throughout Chicago. He had learned his lessons well.

Amongst the criminal élite, Capone was something of a visionary. He viewed crime as big business and ran his organization along strict hierarchical lines, establishing a criminal corporate structure to rival any of America's legitimate companies. The quintessential capitalist, Capone operated his underworld empire with maximum efficiency for maximum profits. He dreamed of uniting the squabbling gangs of Chicago into a single unassailable entity, bringing together Italian, Irish and Jewish mobsters in a common cause. Anyone who questioned his ethics or got in his way was dealt with swiftly and without mercy. Capone's ruthless pursuit of his own personal American Dream led to him being labelled Public Enemy Number 1 by the authorities.

In his private life, Capone remained dedicated to his family and local community. He was a great music lover and became a patron of the arts, using criminal funds to support and promote opera productions in the city. It is unlikely that the history of jazz and blues would have taken quite the same course without Capone's extensive network of music clubs to play host to the pre-eminent musicians and singers of the day. Capone also quietly invested in sporting activities, such as boxing, aware that if word ever got out about his involvement it would cast doubts on the sports' integrity.

Capone's reign as Chicago's criminal kingpin lasted until 1931, when he was arrested and charged with 22 counts of tax evasion as a direct result of a covert operation by a US Treasury agent named Eliot Ness. Although the authorities had tried for years to accuse Capone of some sort of infringement of the law, he had proved an elusive foe, cannily keeping his hands clean of direct involvement in his many crimes and scrupulously covering his tracks afterwards. Then, in 1927, the US Supreme Court set a precedent by convicting a bootlegger named Manny Sullivan for income tax evasion, stating that tax was payable even on criminal enterprises and that, whilst such cases inevitably resulted in self-incrimination, this was not in itself unconstitutional.

Capone was sentenced to imprisonment in the Atlanta State Penitentiary but, in 1934, was moved to the maximum security prison island of Alcatraz off the coast of San Francisco. However, Capone was already entering the tertiary stages of syphilis, which he had contracted in his youth, and was given early release from prison for good behavior in 1939. He spent the next year in a hospital in Baltimore with his wife Mae by his side.

Too ill to ever fully return to his life of crime, Capone retired to his vast estate in Palm Island, Miami, where he died of a heart attack in 1947. He was 48 years old.

Respected by his cohorts, feared by his enemies and loathed by the authorities, Al "Scarface" Capone couldn't help but catch the imagination of the general public. His outrageous exploits were constantly being reported in the national newspapers and this, coupled with his flamboyant lifestyle and insolent demeanour, only served to heighten his glamor and mystique. People began eagerly awaiting his latest transgression, the next twist in his personal mythology.

Of course, there had always been crime in the United States. The Wild West of the 1800s had bred no end of outlaws, desperados and gunslingers whose exploits had been exaggerated and magnified out of all recognition in the public mind. But by the Roaring Twenties, the lawlessness of the pioneer days had achieved a quaint, nostalgic glow. America needed a new breed of anti-hero, part bogeyman and part folk legend, bred out of the poverty and vice of the inner city. It got what it was looking for in the modern-day gangster.

It was inevitable that someone would come along to exploit the reputation of America's mobsters in popular fiction.

That someone was a young writer called Maurice Coons.

2

"Don't toot your horn, honey.
You're not that good."

Elvira Hancock

Scarface was published in 1930, at the very start of what was to become the golden age of hardboiled fiction. The novel's author went by the name of Armitage Trail, the pseudonym of one Maurice Coons.

Coons was born in 1902 and had already established a career as a writer of short fiction by the time he was 18, as a prolific contributor to various pulp magazines. He had lived for a time in the Oak Park district of Chicago and claimed to have intimate knowledge of the gangs that terrorized the city, experience that was later to form the backdrop for *Scarface*. He also hinted that the novel had actually been based on the life of Al Capone. In fact, the events of the novel bore little or no resemblance to Capone's career as a crimelord, but it was a good story to catch the public's attention and sell a few extra copies of his book. Coons's father had been a concert promoter and theatrical impresario, and had obviously instilled in his son the value of publicity and a little ballyhoo.

Scarface is a crude and inelegant novel, whisked up from a queasy mixture of ersatz reportage and lurid pulp melodrama. It has none of the barbed lyricism of Dashiell Hammett, the genuine grit of James M Cain or the tarnished romanticism of Raymond Chandler. The hardboiled dialog, which tries hard to adopt an authentic street patois, is seldom convincing and an unfortunate strain of misogyny runs through the book. ("Being fond, like most blondes, of an easy life secured with the smallest possible expenditure of energy, she obeyed orders" runs one flabbergasting line.)

The novel traces the criminal career of Tony Guarino, a street smart Italian-American 18-year-old who, when the novel opens, is acting as a sometime bagboy for various local hoodlums. Guarino has his own personal motto, of which he reminds the reader repeatedly throughout the book: "I ain't riskin' a pinch for a coupla bucks." He eschews violence towards regular citizens and is scornful of indulging in petty larceny, preferring to use his natural charm to operate various blackmail scams and protection rackets. As he puts it: "What's the use of stickin' people up or bangin' 'em on the head when you can talk 'em out of it?"

When it comes to dealing with fellow criminals, however, Guarino has no moral qualms, even if he gets as giddy as a teenager on the way to the high school prom the moment he gets even a whiff of a cute dame. After falling for brassy burlesque dancer Vyvyan Lovejoy, Guarino recklessly guns down her mobster lover, Al Spingola, which earns him a place in both Lovejoy's tarnished heart and the ranks of Irish crimelord Klondike O'Hara. Adding injury to insult, he also casually punches the local police chief, Captain Flanagan, after he makes an inappropriate comment about Lovejoy in a club. With both the cops and the Spingola gang breathing down his neck, Guarino joins the army and ships out for France, then in the closing stages of World War One.

While fighting in the trenches, Guarino is badly disfigured. "That awful night battle in the woods... had also left him with a long livid scar down the left side of his face, a heavy scar running from the top of his ear to the point of his chin. In some manner the nerves and muscles around his mouth had become involved in the matter and now the left corner of his mouth was drawn upward permanently, not much but it had changed his appearance surprisingly. When he smiled, that corner didn't, and it gave his face an amazingly sinister look."

Guarino comes home a war hero, but his scar means that he is unrecognized even by the members of his own family when he returns to his old stomping grounds (interestingly, Chicago is never mentioned by name in the novel, although the various districts and suburbs of the city described in the text leave no doubt as to the location of the story). He murders Lovejoy in a fit of jealousy when he finds her shacked up with a small-time bootlegger, "Frog" Merlin. Discovering that Klondike O'Hara is now long gone, Guarino takes the name Tony Camonte and insinuates himself into the west side mob run by Johnny Lovo, a smart but unambitious racketeer. He rapidly rises up the ranks of Lovo's gang when he assassinates their north-side rival, Jerry Hoffman. Given his ghastly war wound, it is hardly surprising when he is given the underworld nickname of Scarface.

When Lovo decides to retire, Tony sees his way clear to achieving his ambitions: "He wanted to be a 'big shot', a leader, perhaps a politician. He had a hunger for command, for power, for wealth. And he meant to have it all."

With both the police and the district attorney's office in his pocket, Tony feels free to instigate an all-out gang war against his new north-side rival, "Schemer" Bruno. "I'm going to stop 'em," Tony rages. "If I have to have every man in the mob bumped off. Things have been too quiet lately; from now on they're gonna see action that'll curl their hair." The war reaches a new pitch of ferocity when Bruno begins buying up tommy guns and introducing them into the street fighting. Realizing that the entire city threatens to fall under mob rule, the authorities desperately try to find a way to defuse the situation.

Tony becomes instrumental in his own downfall. When he discovers that his kid sister Rosie is consorting with one of his top gunmen, Mike Rinaldo, Tony walks into their apartment and guns down Rinaldo. It is only later he discovers the pair had secretly been married. With Rosie as a witness, the authorities arrest Camonte and put him on trial for murder, only for him to be acquitted of the killing after bribing the judge. Camonte is desperate for revenge against Captain Flanagan and assistant district attorney Moran for betraying him and assassinates both of them. However, when Rosie subsequently tries to poison him, still blissfully unaware that he is her brother, he simply lets her go.

In a final, unlikely, fit of conscience, Tony writes a confession that implicates the police, local government office and the judiciary in his criminal career, before a brief car chase leads to him being gunned down by his own brother Ben, himself a corrupt cop.

What is most striking about *Scarface* to the modern eye is its cynical depiction of political graft and corruption. There is not a single authority figure in the nove—whether police officer, district attorney, or local judge—who isn't on the take or directly implicated in some criminal venture. By comparison, Tony Guarino operates by a far stronger ethical code: "I keep my word, Steve, whether to friend or enemy, and no matter what I've promised, either good or bad." Tony also justifies his viciousness when dealing with adversaries on the lessons learned during his heroic military service: "Tony's war experience... had taught the younger man such a supreme contempt for human life."

It's hard not to see a censorious editorial hand at work in Tony's last-minute decision to spill the beans about the extent of political corruption in the city: "For the first time in his hectic life he felt the social impulse which is, at once, the cause and result of civilization—the realization that the welfare of mankind was more important than his own preservation, the realization that he owed something to the world." Over the course of the following two hours he pens "the most significantly damning indictment of American political machines ever composed" and it results in "the suicide of half a dozen prominent men, the ruination of innumerable others, a complete reorganization of the government and police administration of not only that city but many others... (it) was to prove the most powerful weapon of modern times for the restoration of decent, dependable government in the larger cities."

The irony of this somewhat pompous attempt to restore public trust in political leaders, which the novel had taken such pains to dismantle over the preceding 24 chapters, is that it also has the effect of transforming Tony into something approaching a martyr. This is reinforced when it is revealed in the novel's closing line that he had not even tried to defend himself when his brother gunned him down.

Not for nothing was it felt by society's moral watchdogs that the rise of "gangster chic" in popular fiction and cinema came dangerously close to glamorizing the outlaw lifestyle rather than condemning it.

The novel of *Scarface* might have been an unsophisticated and exploitative slice of pulp fiction, but it had an eager audience of thrill-seekers awaiting it.

Which was precisely why movie producer Howard Hughes snapped up the rights to the book almost as soon as it was published.

Hughes knew it was gonna make one helluva movie.

3

"He use to take me a lot to the movies…
I watch the guys like Humphrey Bogart, James Cagney.
They teach me to talk. I like those guys."

Tony Montana

Howard Hawks must have been genuinely surprised when Howard Hughes approached him to direct *Scarface*.

At the time, Hughes and Hawks were involved in a bitter lawsuit. Hughes had accused Hawks of stealing material from his World War One flying epic *Hell's Angels* (1930) to use in his movie *The Dawn Patrol* (1930). So when Hawks received word that Hughes wanted him for *Scarface*, he rejected the offer out of hand. It was only when Hughes persisted and offered to drop the lawsuit that Hawks eventually relented.

Despite this fractious beginning to their relationship, the two film-makers got along well and Hawks retained a fond memory of the film. "*Scarface* is my favorite picture, even today," he later admitted. "Because we were completely alone, Hughes and I. Everybody was under contract to the studios. We couldn't get a studio, and they wouldn't loan us anybody, so we had to find a cast. They just didn't want independent pictures made in Hollywood. So we rented a little cobwebbed studio and opened it up and made the picture. It turned out to be the big picture of the year. We didn't get any help from anybody."

Hawks and Hughes had much in common. Both were privileged members of the Hollywood élite, were consummate ladies' men, and shared a love of aviation. At the age of eighteen, Hughes had inherited the prosperous Hughes Tool Company from his father and had used the profits from the manufacture of oil-drilling equipment to fund a number of successful Hollywood movies and invest in his own airline company. Hawks had lived in California from the age of ten and had spent his summers crafting movie props for the Famous Players-Lasky Studio while studying mechanical engineering at Cornell University. It was while making props that he met Douglas Fairbanks and Mary Pickford, who were influential in getting him work as an assistant director. After serving in the Army Air Corps during World War One, Hawks got a job at an aircraft design company, only to quit soon afterwards in order to start working his way up the ladder in the movie business.

Hawks was to become one of Hollywood's most popular and reliable film-makers, and also one of the most versatile. He was adept at virtually every genre: comedy (*Twentieth Century* (1934), *Bringing Up Baby* (1938), and *His Girl Friday* (1940)), drama (*Tiger Shark* (1932), *Come and Get It* (1936), and *Sergeant York* (1941)), thrillers (*To Have and Have Not* (1944) and *The Big Sleep* (1946)), Westerns (*Red River* (1948), *Rio Bravo* (1959), and *El Dorado* (1966)), musicals (*A Song Is Born* (1948) and *Gentlemen Prefer Blondes* (1953)), adventures (*Land of the Pharaohs* (1955) and *Hatari!* (1962)), and even worked uncredited on one horror movie (*The Thing from Another World* (1951), which he also produced.

He never considered himself to be any sort of auteur. "All I'm doing is telling a story. I don't analyze and do a lot of thinking about it. I work on the principle that if I like somebody and think they're attractive, I can make them attractive. If I think a thing's funny, then people laugh at it. If I think a thing's dramatic, the audience does. I'm very lucky that way. I don't stop to analyze it. We just made scenes that were fun to do. I think our job is to make entertainment."

Hawks placed primary importance on a film's script. He once said, "I'm such a coward that unless I get a great writer, I don't want to make a picture."

To adapt the novel of *Scarface* into a screenplay, Hughes had no hesitation in recruiting Ben Hecht, with whom he was also collaborating on a movie adaptation of *The Front Page* (1931), a hit stage play co-written by Hecht and Charles MacArthur.

Hecht was a relatively new arrival in Hollywood. He was already a successful journalist, playwright and novelist living in New York when he received a telegram from fellow writer Herman Mankiewicz in 1926: "Will you accept 300 per week to work for Paramount Pictures? All expenses paid. 300 is peanuts. Millions are to be grabbed out here and your only competition is idiots. Don't let this get around." It was an offer Hecht couldn't refuse.

Moving out to Los Angeles, Hecht's first project was the script for director Josef von Sternberg's *Underworld* (1927), an early crime drama notable for being one of the first to depict life from the gangster's point of view (Howard Hawks always claimed he had collaborated with Hecht on *Underworld*, although this was never corroborated.) The screenplay won Hecht his first Academy Award and he would go on to garner another five nominations, winning again in 1934 for *The Scoundrel*. What set Hecht apart was his lethal wit and golden ear for dialog, transcribed with pinpoint precision.

Throughout his time in Hollywood, Hecht was openly contemptuous of the movie business in general and studio executives in particular, observing, "A movie is never any better than the stupidest man connected with it. There are times when this distinction may be given to the writer or director. Most of time it belongs to the producer." He claimed to be purely in it for the money, frequently not even bothering to claim screen credit for scripts he had reworked for other writers, including *Gone With the Wind* (1939), *Gilda* (1946), *Strangers on a Train* (1951), *Guys and Dolls* (1955), *The Man with the Golden Arm* (1955), and *Cleopatra* (1963). "Hollywood held this double lure for me," he confided. "Tremendous sums of money for work that required no more effort than a game of pinochle."

Hecht reckoned that most of his screenplays took around two weeks to write, eight weeks at the very most.

He dashed off *Scarface* in eleven days.

The first thing Hecht did with Maurice Coons's novel was to throw it out the window.

Hecht's screenplay dispenses with the novel's entire first act, which charted the mobster's fledgling exploits up to his joining the army in World War One. Indeed, the name Tony Guarino is never mentioned in the script; the character is introduced simply as Antonio Camonte (oddly enough, Hecht retains the name Ben Guarino for the cop who has dedicated himself to putting Camonte behind bars, although there is never any suggestion that they are related).

Hecht's Camonte is no fast-talking con man, ladykiller, and former war hero, but a brutal street punk already well-known to the police. Early in the film, having been hauled into police headquarters, he has his rap sheet read out to him: "Assault. Carrying brass knuckles and sap. DW. Disturbing peace. Street robbery on three counts. Loft burglary. Violation of Volstead Act. Indicted for murder of Buck Kempner." A little later, Camonte proudly outlines his personal philosophy: "In this business, there's only one law you've got to follow to keep out of trouble," he impresses on his cohort, Guino "Little Boy" Rinaldo, while miming shooting a pistol. "Do it first, do it yourself, and keep on doing it."

In the opening scene of the script, we find Camonte doing his stuff: cold-bloodedly gunning down gang leader "Big" Louis Costillo in his speakeasy in the aftermath of a wild bachelor party. This brutal assassination allows Camonte to insinuate himself with the weak-willed racketeer Johnny Lovo and help him to assume control of the disorganized west-side gangs, installing himself as Lovo's second-in-command in the process.

At first, Lovo is impressed by Camonte's dedication and cunning. But Camonte's thirst for power knows no bounds and even Lovo becomes alarmed at his ruthless decimation of the rival north-side gang, strong-arming their speakeasies into buying bootleg beer from Lovo's suppliers and systematically killing anyone who gets in his way. Lovo is also infuriated by Camonte's barely-disguised lust for his moll, Poppy. Unknown to Lovo, Poppy is already in the process of switching her allegiances to Camonte.

When the north-side mobster Tom Gaffney ups the ante by importing tommy guns in order to protect his patch, Camonte responds in kind. A gang war breaks out, culminating with Gaffney being gunned down in a bowling alley. In a last-ditch attempt to stop Camonte's inexorable rise to infamy and restore some semblance of order to the city, Lovo tries to arrange his assassination. But the plot fails and Camonte quickly gets his revenge on Lovo, promptly installing himself as the new west-side gang leader.

In one of the few plot elements retained from the original novel, Camonte's eventual downfall begins with him murdering his right-hand man, Guino Rinaldo, whom he believes has led his younger sister Cesca astray, only to discover they had secretly been married. Returning in a daze to his apartment, he finds himself surrounded by the police and, after attempting to shoot his way to freedom, is gunned down in the gutter.

If the shadow of Al Capone is barely visible anywhere in the novel of *Scarface*, he looms large in Hecht's screenplay. Hecht, who had been a newspaperman in Chicago and would have been all too familiar with the backgrounds of the city's most notorious mobsters, adds numerous subtle embellishments to the script that draw direct parallels between Camonte and Capone. In an early scene, when Camonte is being questioned by the police, he is described as being a former member of the Five Points Gang and having relocated from New York to Chicago in 1920, a near accurate match for Capone's tearaway youth and subsequent move to Torrio's patch. A little later, when Camonte tries to shrug off his facial disfigurement with the throwaway line "I

got it in the war," Johnny Lovo responds scornfully, "War...
with a blonde in a Brooklyn speakeasy."

Similarly the key events in Camonte's rise to power
uncannily mirror those of Capone. "Big" Louis Costillo was
based on the real-life figure of Giacomo "Big Jim" Colosimo,
a brothel owner and sometime white slaver, who used his café
as a front for his flesh-peddling business. Once a trusted
cohort of Johnny Torrio, Colosimo later grew greedy and
complacent, and was murdered soon after Capone relocated
to Chicago. Later in the movie, Rinaldo is despatched to
murder the north-side gang leader O'Hara in the florist's
shop which he uses as his headquarters; this is a reference to
one of Capone's great rivals, the Irish mobster Charles Dion
O'Bannion, who did indeed run a successful florist business
and became a casualty in the gang war that gripped Chicago
in the mid-1920s. Likewise, Camonte's bitter enemy Gaffney
is a thinly disguised George "Bugs" Moran, who narrowly
escaped assassination in the St Valentine's Day Massacre
because, like Gaffney, he had been late arriving at the garage
where the hit took place. Hecht never refers to the massacre
by name in the script, although the details of this infamous
mass murder would have been so familiar to the audience of
the day as to make identification unnecessary.

Such sly references were pretty daring for the writer, who
had already experienced one threatening encounter with
Capone over the screenplay. Whilst working on the script,
Hecht told of how he had returned to his hotel room one
night and found two gentlemen from Chicago waiting for
him. They began questioning him, in no uncertain terms, as
to whether it was true that he was working on a movie about

their boss. Hecht tried to placate them by saying that the movie was actually based on the lives of "Big Jim" Colosimo and Charles Dion O'Bannion (a case of Hecht being somewhat economical with the truth). "Then why is the movie called *Scarface*?" the gentlemen asked suspiciously. To which Hecht replied, "If you call the movie *Scarface*, people will think it's about Capone and come to see it. It's part of the racket we call showbusiness." Impressed with his duplicity, the two gentlemen left him to complete the screenplay and returned to Chicago.

(Howard Hawks also reputedly received a visit from half-a-dozen of Capone's goons during the making of the movie. Hawks recounted, "They said, 'The boss wants us to see the picture.' And I said, 'You go and tell him that when it comes out, he can pay a dollar and buy a ticket'.")

The other crucial change between the novel and the screenplay was that all references to police and gubernatorial corruption had been eradicated. Hecht was no fool. He knew that in all of the major cities in which the movie was to play, the local censorship boards were usually affiliated to the city's police force. This was especially true in the key market of New York, where even the inclusion of a scene where an officer of the law was offered a bribe would lead to an instantaneous ban. Had Hecht followed the cynical lead taken by Coons, he would have essentially made the film unplayable anywhere in the United States.

Yet if Hecht thought this would have been enough to placate the censors, he was dead wrong.

At the time that *Scarface* went into production, all movies came under the scrutiny of the Motion Picture Producers and

Distributors of America (MPPDA), a self-regulating board established by the major Hollywood film studios, who had installed the Republican politician and former US Postmaster General Will Hays as its President. The MPPDA—or the Hays Office as it became known—had been created in 1922 to monitor all aspects of film-making in an effort to derail attempts by the government to create a national censorship office. Movies were already subject to the whims of various local censorship bodies and it was felt that the creation of a single government body would be disastrous for the movie industry. If the studios were seen to be keeping their own house in order, it was hoped that the government would leave them alone.

The MPPDA had the power to veto any production as it saw fit, reading every script prior to filming and then scrutinizing the finished film afterwards. It would issue producers with detailed notes as to what was not acceptable and expect them to make the necessary adjustments to ensure that the film was suitable for public consumption. The MPPDA had a long list of taboo subjects, from licentious and drunken behavior to profanity and violence. Since gangster movies, by their very nature, contained just about everything that the MPPDA considered objectionable, they were felt to be high risk ventures for any studio.

Even after the MPPDA had deemed a film suitable for public screening, it could still fall foul of regional or local censorship boards around the United States. In 1932, the year *Scarface* was released, there were seven state censorship boards—Kansas, Maryland, Massachusetts, New York, Ohio, Pennsylvania and Virginia—although many of their neighboring states automatically fell under their jurisdiction. These boards usually charged a fee to view a film and were at liberty to censor anything they chose according to their own whims. Some of these bordered on the farcical. The Pennsylvanian board was obsessed with censoring any references to pregnancy, even something as innocuous as a character knitting baby clothes.

Beyond the state boards, films could also fall prey to the local censorship bodies of various localities. Howard Hughes had been given a rough ride by the censors of Chicago for his 1928 crime drama *The Racket*, about an honest cop's attempts to nail a notorious gangster (loosely based on Al Capone) and encountering government corruption. When mobsters failed in their attempts to use direct threats to get the film stopped during production, they successfully exerted influence on local politicians to have it banned in Chicago.

Hughes was under no illusions about *Scarface*.

He knew that a fight was brewing between him and the censors. He didn't care.

As Hawks observed of his producer: "He'd fight anybody."

Unsurprisingly, when Hughes submitted Hecht's *Scarface* screenplay to the MPPDA for their approval, they sent it back with a long list of changes they deemed necessary to meet their code of conduct.

Hawks and Hecht reluctantly agreed to implement a few of these changes in order to placate the board. One minor adjustment was to the character of Tony Camonte's mother. Her character isn't even mentioned in the novel, but in the initial draft of the script she was portrayed as a "grasping virago" in the MPPDA's words. They felt that such a portrayal would draw fire from the Italian-American community. Hecht rewrote her part as an almost total cliché, the long-suffering mother wringing her hands over her ne'er-do-well son.

In line with the MPPDA's recommendations, Hecht agreed to bolster up the characters of the law enforcers on Camonte's trail. He penned a lengthy and tiresomely portentous speech for the police commissioner which condemned the gangster lifestyle. "They had some excuse for glorifying our old Western bad men," he intones. "They met in the middle of the street at high noon and waited for each other to draw. But these 'things' sneak up on a man and shoot him in the back... When I think what goes on in the minds of these lice, I want to vomit."

However, not all of the changes wrought at the MPPDA's behest were to be to the detriment of the finished film. Particularly the resolution to the problem of Camonte's sister, Cesca.

Hecht and Hawks had been given strict instructions by the MPPDA to contrive a less sympathetic relationship between Camonte and Cesca. Throughout the script, Camonte had been depicted as a staunch family man obsessed with defending his sister's honor. The censors were most concerned about the scene immediately following Rinaldo's murder, when Cesca appears from the shadows of Camonte's apartment, intent on avenging his death. Notwithstanding the fact that her brother has just murdered her husband, Cesca has a last-minute change of heart, lowers her gun and instead conspires to help Camonte escape from the surrounding police.

Irritated by what they considered to be a ludicrous request by the MPPDA, Hawks and Hecht impudently took the board at their word and made the siblings' relationship less sympathetic... by implying that Camonte harbored incestuous longings for his sister. They later claimed to have retooled the characters to resemble Cesare and Lucrezia Borgia, a daring conceit for 1932. Consider this shockingly suggestive (for the time) exchange after Camonte finds Cesca fraternizing with a young man and forbids her from seeing him again:

Camonte: "Listen, I don't want anyone kissing my sister, understand."

Cesca: "You're hurting my arm."

Camonte: "I don't want anyone putting their hands on you."

Cesca: "What do you think *you're* doing?"

Camonte: "I'm your brother."

Cesca: "You don't act it. You act more like... I don't know. Sometimes I think..."

Camonte: "I don't care what you think."

This twisted relationship becomes even more brazen later on, when Camonte encounters Cesca in a speakeasy, dancing cheek-to-cheek with a lounge lizard. He drags her home and, in a symbolic act of rape, brutally rips apart one of the straps holding up her dress, exposing her brassiered breast. In the final scene, Cesca has completed the transformation from giggly good time girl to vampish black widow, gleefully egging her brother on to his doom until she gets caught in the crossfire. It's worth pointing out that the image of Camonte weeping over Cesca's corpse would become the only tender moment in the entire film.

So Hughes, Hecht and Hawks won a few battles and they lost a few battles with the MPPDA. Throughout all of this, however, the trio were adamant on one thing: they were not going to change the film's ending.

The explosive grand finale of *Scarface* was the element of the screenplay over which the MPPDA had expressed their deepest concern.

In the ending of the script, Camonte was to make a break for freedom from his apartment and find his path blocked by Ben Guarino, the police detective who had been on his trail for the entire movie. Camonte was to shoot and kill Guarino, and then be mown down in a hail of gunfire from the police. The MPPDA thought that Guarino's murder not only signified a partial victory of evil over good, but also that Camonte meeting his own death without a shred of remorse glamorized his character to an unacceptable degree. They insisted that not only must Guarino be allowed to survive, but that Camonte also be depicted as more cowardly in the closing moments of the film.

Howard Hughes agreed with Hawks and Hecht that the ending of the film should remain as scripted, but was concerned that continuing to argue their case with the MPPDA would only delay the film still further. He was well aware that at least two other major gangster movies were already in production—*The Public Enemy* at Warner Brothers and *Little Caesar* at First National Pictures—and was determined to get *Scarface* onto movie screens first.

"Screw the Hays Office," he instructed Hawks. "Start the picture and make it as realistic, as exciting, as grisly as possible."

4

"I need a guy with steel in his balls.
I need him close to me."

Frank Lopez

Because most of the major Hollywood studios were unwilling to lend out any of their contract players for Hughes's independent production, he was forced to cast his net wider. Howard Hawks traveled to New York to see if he could find any Broadway actors he could cast in the movie.

He returned with Paul Muni.

At the time he was cast in *Scarface*, Muni was already one of the most distinguished theater actors in America. Born in Austria in 1897, he had emigrated with his parents to America and was raised in New York City then Cleveland. He got his first stage role with the Yiddish Theater in New York in 1907, but was not to appear in an English-language role until 1926. He had some experience of working in Hollywood, where he earned the distinction of being one of the few actors to be nominated for an Academy Award for Best Actor in his screen debut, an adaptation of the one-act play *The Valiant* (1929).

Muni was to earn a second Best Actor nomination for his hard-edged performance as wrongly accused convict James Allen in *I Am a Fugitive from a Chain Gang* (1932), but only walked away with one of the coveted statuettes for playing the title role of the celebrated chemist in *The Story of Louis Pasteur* (1935). Despite his remarkable range as an actor, Muni had taken no formal acting lessons and eschewed any method in his performances. "I've never tried to learn the art of acting," he once admitted. "I've been in the business for years but I still can't tell what acting is or how it's done." Similarly, he had no time for the trappings of stardom: "I think 'star' is what you call actors who can't act."

It was Muni's physical capabilities that attracted Hawks. He'd caught a performance in New York where the 33-year-old actor had convincingly played an old man. "Muni could do any damn thing you'd tell him to do," Hawks enthused.

Early in his career, Muni had been dubbed "The New Lon Chaney" because of his uncanny ability to transform himself physically for a role. This was exactly the quality that Hawks was looking for. Far from wanting to glamorize the gangster, Hawks wanted to dehumanize him. He wanted Tony Camonte to appear almost sub-normal and ape-like, as if he had regressed one step back down the evolutionary ladder. To distance Camonte from normal society even more, Hawks went much farther than Maurice Coons in disfiguring the character. Camonte's scar now not only stretched from his cheekbone down to his jawline, but a second scar bisected it, running horizontally from the bridge of his nose to his ear, forming a vivid X.

Standing just 70 inches, Paul Muni was not a particularly imposing figure. To help the actor appear more intimidating, lifts were placed in his shoes that raised him another three or four inches. His costumes were also padded to give him additional bulk. When Muni adopted a cocky swagger and an ironic smile, the portrait was complete.

Yet while he might have looked the part, Muni was not, at heart, a tough guy. He was a very quiet, self-possessed person and had never been in a real fight in his life. Hawks had to ask a boxer friend to coach Muni in the art of throwing a punch. As Hawks recounted: "For a couple of weeks, he'd put his hand up and Muni would hit it. When we filmed the scene, the fellow started with his hand up and then took his hand away and took the punch. Muni just stood there staring at him. I said 'Act, you son of a bitch! Act!'"

In the finished film, Muni's Camonte is vain, arrogant, slow-witted, and untrustworthy, yet not without a certain animal magnetism. Even by today's standards, his character comes across as believably unhinged, a wild beast eager and capable of indulging in any whim, no matter how perverse. The sequence where he lovingly fondles his tommy gun with childlike glee and blurts, "Get out of my way, Johnny! I'm gonna spit!" is one of the cinema's earliest and most memorable instances of firearm fetishism.

Hawks confirmed that this infantile aspect of Camonte's character had been intentional. "A great many of the gangsters I met *were* pretty childish. I get awfully sick and tired of a lot of the gangster stuff that I see where everybody is growling at somebody and being the toughest guy in the world. These fellows were not that way. They were just like kids."

The film-makers themselves also got to indulge their more childish natures. When Howard Hughes saw the rushes of one of Hawks's big stunts, wherein a truck crashes after being forced off the road by machine-gun fire, he got wildly excited. "My God, that was a good one! Why don't you make some more of 'em?" The crew ended up staging nineteen automotive crashes for the movie.

The rest of the *Scarface* cast was made up of stage actors like Osgood Perkins (father of Anthony Perkins), who played Johnny Lovo, Karen Morley, who appeared as Poppy, and C Henry Gordon, who played Ben Guarino. Boris Karloff, who appeared as the mobster Gaffney, had yet to appear in *Frankenstein* (1931) the film that would transform him into a household name and typecast him for the rest of his career. Vince Barnett made his film debut in the movie as Tony's "secretary" Angelo, taking a break from his regular job as a party clown. Ann Dvorak, who played Cesca, was a chorus girl and choreographer at MGM pictures and one of the only cast members on loan for the film; Hawks liked her so much that he also cast her in his next picture, *The Crowd Roars* (1932). Hawks himself made a brief cameo appearance as the doomed mobster Meehan.

By far the cleverest coup was in casting George Raft in the pivotal role of Tony Camonte's trusted cohort, Guino "Little Boy" Rinaldo. Although he barely has more than a couple of dozen lines in the movie, Raft's laconic presence at the edge of the screen, casually flipping a coin, transformed him into a superstar. It helped that Raft, who had been pally with the mobsters Benjamin "Bugsy" Siegel and Owney Madden during his youth in New York's Hell's Kitchen district, had long been reputed to have even stronger ties to organized crime. Raft never really confirmed or denied these rumors, which just served to heighten his mystique even further. He had originally come to Hollywood as a bit player and dancer, but after *Scarface* he became one of the screen's most iconic tough guys.

Hawks's abiding memory of the film was that it had been a genuinely collaborative experience, with none of the problems associated with having a big studio breathing down his neck. "That picture was a lot of fun," he reminisced. "Everybody in the crew would try to think of something that would happen. Every member of the crew played a part in it. They really enjoyed the fact that they were independent."

The MPPDA were not pleased when Howard Hughes sent them the completed print of *Scarface* for their approval. Howard Hawks had completely disregarded their instructions and proceeded to shoot the film's ending exactly as Ben Hecht had scripted it. The MPPDA insisted it had to be changed: Ben Guarino had to be allowed to survive and Tony Camonte had to be depicted as a complete coward.

Hughes and Hawks thought the suggestion that Camonte "turn yellow" was patently ridiculous given everything that had preceded it. They were prepared to allow Guarino to survive, but only if the film otherwise ended as they had filmed it. Hawks attempted to make them see reason: "I made a scene where he ended up in the gutter, in a pile of horse manure, and I said 'Isn't that enough?'"

After much arguing, the MPPDA suggested a compromise that the film-makers reluctantly agreed upon. Camonte would be disarmed by Guarino in their final encounter and be forced to plead for his life, thus proving Guarino's earlier allegation that Camonte was a born coward: "Take your gun away, get you in a tough spot and you'll squeal, like all the other rats." Then, at the last minute, Camonte would make a run for it and get shot down.

With all parties now in agreement, Hawks went back and reshot the ending.

Production wrapped on *Scarface* and the film was made ready for release. It was months behind schedule as a result of all the censorship problems, but at least the film-makers had finally secured the MPPDA's approval.

Or so it seemed.

All of the negotiations concerning *Scarface* had so far been conducted between the film-makers and Jason S Joy, who was head of the MPPDA's Public Relations Committee in Hollywood. It was only after the ending had been reshot that it was sent to New York and screened for the President of the organization, Will Hays. And Hays was mortified.

Hays contacted Howard Hughes and told him that he considered *Scarface* to unreleasable in its present form. He demanded that Hughes shoot a completely new "moral" ending in which Camonte was arrested, forced to stand trial and summarily executed. He also demanded that the film include additional scenes in which it is made plain that most Italian-Americans are uninvolved with organized crime and which promoted a much stronger anti-gun message. And he demanded that the title be changed.

Howard Hawks, Ben Hecht and Paul Muni had all moved on to other projects and refused to implement any more changes. It was left to Hughes to get writer Fred Pasley to script the additional scenes and revised ending, which were then directed by Richard Rosson using a stand-in for Paul Muni. This body double was only filmed from behind or from a distance in order to mask his true identity. A disclaimer was added to the start of the movie which talks about the need for gun control. The film's title was changed to *The Shame of a Nation*. Until, that is, it was discovered that someone else held the copyright for that title, after which it was changed back to *Scarface* again.

When the film was finally released, over a year after its scheduled release date, it was still banned by numerous local censorship boards as a result of its explicit violence. Amusingly, the revised "moral" ending insisted upon by Will Hays had to be replaced with the original immoral ending for certain districts which had specific laws that forbade the depiction of scenes of execution. Nowadays, *Scarface* is seldom screened with Rosson's hastily contrived alternative ending, although most prints still include his other sequences—most notably, a stilted conversation between a newspaper editor and various concerned citizens about the ethics of reporting on mob activity—clumsily inserted into the main flow of the story.

Although Howard Hawks later claimed that *Scarface* had been a colossal success when it was released in theaters in 1932, in truth it only performed modestly at the box office. Both *Little Caesar* and *The Public Enemy* had been huge hits the previous year, but audiences displayed little enthusiasm for Tony Camonte's brand of celluloid psychopathy.

Howard Hughes, who had been forced to spend a small fortune on costly reshoots and had watched the film's budget skyrocket to almost $1 million, ended up making only a tiny profit from his gangster epic.

One person, however, never lived to see *Scarface* on the big screen. The author Maurice Coons had moved out to

Hollywood when *Scarface* had been optioned, obviously looking to expand into screenwriting. He had been grossly overweight for many years and he collapsed from a fatal heart attack in the foyer of the Paradise Theater in Los Angeles in 1930. He was just 28 years old.

5

"I always tell the truth. Even when I lie."

Tony Montana

Howard Hawks was one of Hollywood's most celebrated raconteurs. But even his friends knew better than to take his stories without a pinch of salt. Ben Hecht described him as being perpetually "a-purr with melodrama."

There was an amusing story that Howard Hawks always liked to recount about *Scarface*: "A famous gangster brought two very lovely daughters out to watch the movie and introduced himself to me. He said 'Where'd you get the stuff on that killing?' I asked him 'Why? Are you mad?' He said 'No, I'm just curious.' So I told him and he laughed, and he said 'That's the way we did the shooting. Why hasn't the picture played in Chicago?' I said 'They won't let me.' He said 'Do you *want* it to play?' I said 'Yeah.' And he said 'Can I use your phone a minute?' When he was finished, he said 'You can play it any time you want.'"

Scarface became the gangster's gangster picture. Hawks later confided that he had been issued an invitation to go and meet Al Capone just so that the mobster could tell him how much he liked the movie. Capone even bought his own print of the film and screened it regularly for his cronies. Many years later, after the death of the Chicago mob boss Sam Giancana in 1975, it was reported that amongst Sam's possessions was a small custom-made globe bearing the slogan "The World is Yours", just like the Cook's Tours sign outside Tony Camonte's apartment window.

Whilst most of the other gangster movies of the era have dated and seem more than a little quaint to modern moviegoers, *Scarface* still packs a punch more than 70 years since its original release. One can only imagine how brutal it must have seemed to audiences of the time. Even its opening scene, where a janitor quizzically plucks a discarded brassiere from amongst the strewn decorations of Louis Costillo's bachelor party, must have been daringly risqué for 1930s moviegoers. The language throughout is harsh and guttural, the violence is casual and unremitting, the tone is amoral and pessimistic. It seems hardly surprising that when the UK censors took another look at the film for its home video release in 1986, they still deemed it only suitable for viewers over the age of 15.

What is also remarkable about the film is its stylishness. Howard Hawks was a film-maker who was generally more absorbed by dialog and performances than by tricky camera moves and inventive action sequences. Yet in *Scarface*, the camerawork is fluid and kinetic, and the film is stuffed full of explosive set pieces such as the lengthy tommy gun attack on the Columbia Café.

There is also a fascinating visual motif running through the film that utilizes light and shade in a way that predates the advances in cinematography pioneered by the great film noir directors. With each transgression committed by Tony Camonte, a vivid X appears on screen, mirroring the lurid slashes across the mobster's scarred face. In the opening scene, the X appears on an interior glass partition in Louis Costillo's café, through which Camonte can be seen murdering the mobster in silhouette. It appears as a shadow on the wall above Meehan's hospital bed as Camonte bursts through the doors to assassinate him. Immediately following the St Valentine's Day Massacre sequence, the camera pans up to the Xs formed by a girder supporting the ceiling of the garage. Sometimes these Xs are almost subliminal, such as the strike marked on Gaffney's scorecard just before he is gunned down in the bowling alley or the spaghetti straps across the back of Cesca's evening gown before Camonte tears the dress from her shoulder.

It's like a sly wink from the director to the audience.

A wink that says that *Scarface* was, and always would be, X-rated material.

part two:

cutting edge

6

"All I have in this world is my balls and my word.
And I don't break them for no one."

Tony Montana

"All of the films I have made with Al," Martin Bregman maintains, "I have created for him. Specifically for him. Specifically things which he could do best."

Having piqued Pacino's interest with the idea of a reconceptualized *Scarface*, Bregman had approached Universal Pictures, which had bought the rights to the property after the death of Howard Hughes, and been given their blessing to develop a remake.

This was his baby. Now he just had to nurture it into existence.

The logical choice as director for the project would have been Sidney Lumet.

Bregman and Pacino had worked with Lumet on both *Serpico* and *Dog Day Afternoon*. They worked well together. They understood each other. They had a rapport. Lumet was a serious film-maker who didn't shy away from controversial material. He was experienced, reliable and well respected. And he was bankable.

Yet there was another film-maker who Bregman had his eye on: Brian De Palma.

In the ten years since he had arrived in Hollywood, De

Palma had established himself as one of his generation's premier movie stylists. He had a brilliant eye for detail and was a genius at staging hugely complex set pieces with apparent ease. He was also one of the few directors who really understood and respected genre cinema, who was trying to propel it towards new levels of sophistication.

That appealed to Bregman. He had described *Scarface* as "a gangster opera" where everything was to be larger than life: heightened performances, heightened emotions, and heightened action.

He thought that Brian De Palma was just the director to pull it off.

When Brian De Palma arrived in Hollywood in 1970, he was instantly assimilated into the group of young film-makers who were to change the face of the film industry. The Young Turks. The New Hollywood. The Movie Brats.

Within the decade, Steven Spielberg, George Lucas, Martin Scorsese, Francis Ford Coppola and Brian De Palma would all become household names.

Depending, of course, on what sort of household you lived in...

Unlike the other members of his circle, De Palma's first love had not been the cinema. Whereas most of the Movie Brats had grown up on a diet of movies and more movies, De Palma was the son of an orthopedic surgeon and had spent his youth watching his father perform operations, filling up his spare time by tinkering with mechanical experiments and designing computers.

"I was one of those science types who was always up in his

room with all these parts," De Palma once admitted. "I was brought up in the 1950s when going to the moon was the most important thing a man would ever do." It is an open secret that the Keith Gordon role in *Dressed To Kill*, the lonely nerd who is desperate to solve his mother's murder, is the closest the director has come to depicting himself on screen.

It was only while studying for his degree in physics and technology at Columbia University, that De Palma became absorbed by cinema, in particular the films of Alfred Hitchcock, Luis Buñuel and Jean-Luc Godard. "I traded one obsession for another," he said. Having already been active in the campus theater scene, De Palma began writing and shooting short films. The most successful of these, *Wotan's Wake*, won the Rosenthal Foundation award, given for the best short film by a film-maker under the age of 25, in 1962.

Upon graduating from Columbia, De Palma won a writing fellowship at Sarah Lawrence College and it was here that he made his first feature film, *The Wedding Party*, in 1964. For this improvisatory comedy, De Palma called on the services of his various friends and fellow students, including future stars Jill Clayburgh and Robert De Niro. The film also featured performances by De Palma's close friends William Finley and Jennifer Salt.

The Wedding Party did not get a theatrical release until 1969, by which time De Palma had completed two further features, *Murder à la Mod* (1968) and *Greetings* (1968). If *The Wedding Party* had already demonstrated De Palma's love of film experimentation with its elaborate scenes in slow and fast motion as well as disorienting jump cuts, *Murder à la Mod* revealed him to also be a master of pastiche. This *Rashomon-*

style tale of a murder seen from three different perspectives depicts each section in a different cinematic style: melodrama, slapstick comedy, and, in an early indication of things to come, Hitchcockian suspense. *Greetings*, on the other hand, was an anarchic comedy very much in line with the counterculture and once again featured Robert De Niro.

De Palma completed two more films in New York. The first was a film of a 1969 stage production of the play *Dionysus*, titled appropriately enough *Dionysus in 69* (1970), which made extensive use of split screen to show both actors and audience simultaneously. This was followed by *Hi Mom!* (1970), a sort-of sequel to *Greetings* focusing on the experiences of the Robert De Niro character after he returns from the Vietnam War.

De Palma's modestly successful movies had not gone unnoticed on America's west coast. Hollywood was undergoing its own revolution following the cult success of *Easy Rider* (1969) and studio executives were snapping up any screenplays that promised to speak to the youth market. Warner Brothers invited De Palma to direct a vehicle for the comedian Tom Smothers entitled *Get To Know Your Rabbit*, revolving around a meek corporate drone who decides to become a stage magician. De Palma accepted their offer and made his way to Hollywood, unaware that the experience was to end in disaster.

"In Hollywood you set the perimeters of your own destruction," De Palma said of his experiences on *Get To Know Your Rabbit*. "I learned what I couldn't control and what I could. I learned you can't overcome certain things that you are strapped with right from the beginning. You can only work within the system if you have a strong enough power base and can control all the elements around you."

For De Palma, fresh from the east coast and working on his first major studio production, *Get To Know Your Rabbit* amounted to a series of clashes. He clashed with screenwriter Jordan Crittenden over rewrites of the script and the ending of the film. He clashed with the Warner executives who refused to entertain some of his more experimental ideas, such as incorporating 16mm footage into the film (Head of Production John Calley succinctly said "Brian De Palma was a monster"). And whilst, on the surface, De Palma felt he had the full support of Tom Smothers, he later claimed the film's star had "stabbed me in the back." De Palma was sacked from the movie, other hands were brought in to do reshoots, the film was recut and then sat on the shelf for six months. It received a brief theatrical release in 1972 and has seldom been screened since.

The fiasco over *Get To Know Your Rabbit*, however, gave De Palma a certain cachet amongst his fellow film-makers. The prevailing feeling amongst them was that they were rebels, ready to conquer all in their stride. As Martin Scorsese put it "We were fighting to open up the form... We weren't equipped to shoot in studios, didn't come from the studio tradition."

As writer Peter Biskind pointed out in his book *Easy Riders, Raging Bulls*, the beach house which Jennifer Salt shared with fellow actor Margot Kidder became the unofficial hang-out of De Palma's friends. Lucas, Spielberg, and Scorsese, John Milius, Paul Schrader, Walter Hill; anyone and everyone. It was the Movie Brats' playpen, a place to share dreams, swap notes, and eye up the opposition. De Palma was already the most experienced film-maker of the group, with six feature films under his belt. He was also something of a ladies' man. As Kidder, by then his girlfriend, observed "Brian was the guy all the guys wanted to be."

Privately, De Palma had been disappointed and demoralized by the run-in with Warner Brothers. In the fallout from *Get To Know Your Rabbit*, the only film he had been offered was an adaptation of *Fuzz*, one of the 87th Precinct crime novels written by Ed McBain. De Palma had expressed enthusiasm for the project and managed to get Burt Reynolds on board as NYPD Detective Steve Carella. But when United Artists threatened to withdraw funding unless De Palma agreed to also cast the wholly inappropriate Raquel Welch and Yul Brynner in the film, he withdrew from the production.

But he continued writing.

In December 1971, De Palma wrapped up two copies of a screenplay and gave them to Margot Kidder and Jennifer Salt as a Christmas present. It was the script for a quirky thriller entitled *Sisters* which he had written with them in mind. Kidder was to play a pair of formerly conjoined twins, with Salt as the journalist who inadvertently witnesses one of the twins committing a murder. There was also a role for De Palma's old college friend, William Finley.

Independent producer Edward R Pressman scraped together the money to put *Sisters* into production, allegedly from the profits of his family's toymaking business, and De Palma was given the freedom to indulge his obsession with Hitchcock. Shot on a budget of under $1 million, the film is crammed with references to *Rear Window* (1954) and *Psycho* (1960), with a dash of Roman Polanski's *Repulsion* (1965) thrown in for good measure. De Palma also employed numerous feints with the film's narrative and applied stylistic devices such as split screen to alternately engross and disorient the audience. And he was finally able to try out his experiment of mixing 35mm and 16mm footage which he had been denied on *Get To Know Your Rabbit*. The final icing on the cake was in tracking down Bernard Herrmann, the composer most associated with Hitchcock, in London and getting him to score the film. Although De Palma found Herrmann a demanding and abrasive character, his lavish orchestral score, at turns dreamlike and nightmarish, brought a touch of class to the low budget production.

When *Sisters* was released in 1973 it immediately caught the attention of the mainstream critics. The *Los Angeles Times* dubbed it "A triumph... a richly detailed exercise in mounting fear and suspense" while the *San Francisco Examiner* described it as "slick, fast-paced, imaginative and scary" and *Time* praised the "delicate balance between humor and horror". In the UK, *Sisters* was released as *Blood Sisters* and slipped out on the lower half of a double bill with the werewolf whodunit *The Beast Must Die* (1974) from Amicus Productions.

After the success of *Sisters*, Ed Pressman had no hesitation in financing De Palma's next feature, a horror musical loosely based on the legend of Faust and incorporating plot elements from Gaston Leroux's *Phantom of the Opera*. The script had actually been written at the same time as *Sisters* and was then entitled *Phantom of the Fillmore*. It was only once the film was in production that De Palma discovered he would be unable to use the name of the legendary east and west coast rock venues, so the title was changed to *Phantom of the Paradise*. Songwriter and sometime actor Paul Williams was brought in to both compose the movie's soundtrack and appear as the demonic music mogul, Swan.

From the outset, De Palma played down the horror elements of the story in favor of a more fantastical approach. He seemed to be courting the audience that had embraced Richard O'Brien's camp stage musical *The Rocky Horror Show* and The Who's rock opera *Tommy*. For the scene in which William Finley, who plays the film's anti-hero Winslow Leach, has his face crushed in a record press and subsequently transforms himself into the Phantom, De Palma chose to downplay the gore. "I had originally included a longer look on Finley's face, all bloody and steaming, after he came off the record press," De Palma explained. "But I thought it was too excessive for the movie."

When *Phantom* was completed, 20th Century Fox bought the rights to distribute the movie for $2 million, setting a new record for the amount paid for an independent feature. They were obviously expecting it to be a huge success. Instead, the film got off to a shaky start at the box office mainly because of a misleading publicity campaign. "We originally used a piece of artwork which made everyone think it was some kind of rock or concert film like *Gimme Shelter* (1970) or *Woodstock* (1970), which was a big mistake," said De Palma, before admitting "I went along with everyone else, thinking that would be its audience." It was only after the advertising was modified to emphasize the more fantastical aspects of the story that it slowly began to develop a cult following. Nevertheless the damage had been done and the film failed to repeat the financial success of *Sisters*.

Having been attempting to edge away from the horror genre with *Phantom of the Paradise*, De Palma abandoned it entirely for his next picture, *Obsession*.

Obsession had been put together by De Palma and screenwriter Paul Schrader over the course of a single afternoon. De Palma wanted to make a more serious homage to Hitchcock than he had with *Sisters* and, in particular, to the film that had enraptured him at university, *Vertigo*. To this, Schrader combined thematic elements from one of his own favorite films, Yasujiro Ozu's *An Autumn Afternoon* (1962). Together they thrashed out a detailed story outline: a businessman is haunted by the death of his wife and daughter in a botched kidnapping, for which he feels partly responsible. Many years later, he returns to the place where he first met his wife and chances upon a woman who looks exactly like her. At which point, history creepily begins to repeat itself.

The subsequent script went through numerous title changes, including *Déjà Vu* and *Double Ransom*, before De Palma and Schrader settled on *Obsession*. Working with cinematographer Vilmos Zsigmond on location in New Orleans and Florence, De Palma transformed the screenplay into a florid romantic melodrama that owed as much to Hitchcock's *Rebecca* as to *Vertigo*. The film was, once again, dominated by a lush, rhapsodic score from Bernard Herrmann. De Palma also, without Schrader's knowledge, made radical changes to the ending of the story and the writer was so upset he threatened to remove his name from the credits.

Obsession was a critical success and, against the odds for such an old fashioned and seemingly uncommercial movie, a modest box-office hit. It was also selected to be screened in competition at the Cannes Film Festival. Yet despite all of this attention and acclaim, De Palma's career failed to gather any momentum and he was still struggling to interest studios in his projects.

Having, at one time, been "the guy that all the guys wanted to be", De Palma was being left behind. Coppola hit big with *The Godfather* (1972), Lucas with *American Graffiti* (1973), and Spielberg with *Jaws* (1975). They were the guys De Palma wanted to be.

He wanted a hit movie.

And he found one.

7

"You know what capitalism is? Getting fucked."

Tony Montana

In 1973, a former high school teacher from Maine took the only copy of a short story he had been writing, screwed it up and threw it in the bin. He had decided that the story wasn't working and he was unsure how to proceed. The writer had managed to sell a few short stories in the past, mainly to pulp and girlie magazines, and had made four attempts at a novel, none of which had sold. He supported himself and his wife by working in a laundry.

It was only later that his wife retrieved the story from the bin and gave it a read. When he returned home she suggested he take another look at it. "You've got something here," she told him.

The writer was Stephen King. And the manuscript his wife Tabitha had saved from destruction was the opening section of a novel that would eventually be entitled *Carrie*, the tale of a persecuted high-school misfit who vents her rage on her despised classmates using her ferocious telekinetic powers. *Carrie* was published in 1974 and became the cornerstone of Stephen King's writing career: it would transform him into one of America's bestselling novelists.

De Palma didn't get around to reading *Carrie* until 1975, but was immediately attracted to the story. "I read the book and said 'I know how to make this,' and then sought out the people who owned it and basically begged for the job."

One of De Palma's dream projects since the 1960s had been to make a screen adaptation of a book that had captured his imagination in his youth, Alfred Bester's seminal science fiction novel *The Demolished Man* (1953). This speculative thriller is set in a society where telepathic police are pursuing a murderer who has managed to find a way around their invasive paranormal abilities. The conclusion of the story has a cop literally invading the killer's mind, to strip away the protective layers and expose his guilt.

De Palma had already made several attempts to write a screenplay based on the novel, but knew it would be a difficult property to get into production. With its futuristic scenario and complex psychological nature, the film would be heavily reliant on special effects and De Palma wasn't so naïve as to think that any studio would entrust him with the sort of colossal budget required to get such a demanding story up on the screen. *Carrie*, however, encompassed many of the themes that had so intrigued him in *The Demolished Man*, except with a far more straightforward plot and less of a reliance on complex special effects.

Having discovered that the rights to *Carrie* were owned by producer Paul Monash, he petitioned heavily for the job. Monash wasn't keen on the idea of hiring De Palma, but had already struck a deal to make the movie with United Artists who gave the director their support. "I had to beg for the job. I pleaded, *pleaded*, to be allowed to direct it. Frankly, I was more than ready for big-time success. All my best friends in the business—Martin Scorsese, George Lucas, Steven

Spielberg—had already made it in a huge way, and there I was, after eight or nine pictures, still struggling." Monash eventually gave his assent.

De Palma held auditions for *Carrie* in collaboration with George Lucas, who was trying to find actors for an upcoming project entitled *The Star Wars* (it was only later that Lucas's film lost its definite article). It was ironic that, at the time, *Carrie* was by far the hotter of the two properties.

De Palma and Lucas swapped notes in between auditions and many of the actors who lost out on roles in Lucas's space opera found parts in De Palma's horror flick. Amy Irving had been a strong contender for the role of Princess Leia Organa in *The Star Wars* and William Katt had been considered for Han Solo. When Lucas passed on the pair, De Palma gave both of them roles in *Carrie*. He also cast John Travolta, then best known for his role as Vinnie Barberini in the TV sitcom *Welcome Back, Kotter*, and Nancy Allen, who would later become De Palma's wife. He was also surprised to discover that Piper Laurie, who had quit the movies after her Oscar-nominated performance in *The Hustler* in 1961, was willing to come out of retirement for the movie.

Carrie would go on to become De Palma's biggest hit to date and one of the most profitable movies of 1976. Made for just $1.8 million, it went on to take more than $33 million at the US box office alone. It also earned Academy Award nominations for Sissy Spacek in the title role and for Piper Laurie as her suffocatingly evangelical mother.

De Palma finally had his hit, but it didn't make his professional life any easier.

After his success with *Carrie*, De Palma was pressed against his better judgment into handling another psychic thriller, *The Fury*, based on the novel by John Farris. De Palma wasn't all that enamoured with the storyline, but hoped, at the very least, that the film would prove he could handle a big budget and big name stars.

But it didn't work out that way.

The Fury was budgeted at $5.5 million, a major step up for De Palma, and starred a genuine cinema legend in Kirk Douglas. Whilst it was a modestly successful movie, it wasn't well liked by either critics or fans. The script written by John Farris was confusing and sluggish, and while De Palma brought his usual visual flair to the piece, the film seemed more like a collection of stylish set pieces than an organic story. Whereas the gore in *Sisters* and *Carrie* had been sparingly used and all the more effective for it, *The Fury*'s grisly special effects became the film's whole *raison d'être*. Walking out of the movie, the only memorable aspect of the whole sorry endeavour was John Cassavetes being psychically blown to smithereens in the final shot.

To further compound De Palma's woes, he also found himself on the receiving end of some of the worst notices of his career. The very critics who had supported him for most of his early films found *The Fury* to be crass and pointless. It was just another anonymous Hollywood blockbuster, devoid of any real style, content or humanity. Critic Leonard Maltin was not alone when he dismissed it as "The ultimate litmus test for those who prefer form over content."

There was more disappointment to come.

After *The Fury*, De Palma wanted to get as far away from horror movies as possible, shelving *The Demolished Man* for the time being; three psychic thrillers in a row would have finished off his career for good.

He found a kindred spirit in actor John Travolta, who had become a teen heartthrob thanks to *Welcome Back, Kotter* and the hit disco dance drama *Saturday Night Fever* (1977), but was looking to expand his range. People remembered Travolta strutting his stuff on the dance floor in his iconic white suit in *Fever*, but hadn't registered that he had given an impressively nuanced performance as Tony Manero in the movie. That summer's big hit movie, *Grease* (1978), had kept Travolta in the limelight, but done precious little to enhance his credibility as an actor. Furthermore, Travolta had turned down a prestigious role in Terrence Malick's *Days of Heaven* (1978), only for it to give a huge boost to the career of Richard Gere. (Travolta would continue to promote Gere's rise to superstardom by also turning down the leads in Paul Schrader's *American Gigolo* (1980) and Taylor Hackford's *An Officer and a Gentleman* (1982).)

De Palma had begun work on the script for a police drama entitled *Prince of the City*, which he also planned to direct and for which he thought Travolta would be perfect as the lead. The story was a fictionalized account of the story of Bob Leuci, a corrupt NYPD cop who had betrayed his colleagues by helping the authorities expose corruption in the police force. This was to be De Palma's big breakthrough—a serious, quality drama on an important topic. He was co-writing the screenplay with playwright David Rabe, in close collaboration with Leuci himself.

Even while he was touring round the world promoting *The Fury*, *Prince of the City* was uppermost in De Palma's mind. "This is not a project that I'm preparing and going to send to John Travolta. He was involved in it right from the beginning, as I was," he said at the time.

Then Orion Pictures, for whom he was developing *Prince of the City*, abruptly fired him from the project.

In De Palma's eyes, he was betrayed by the Orion executives: "I worked on that movie for a year and a half... and they didn't like my approach to the material. They felt more comfortable with Sidney Lumet. With Sidney Lumet, they could get it co-financed by Warner Brothers. He's a very good director, but I believed they were basically protecting their downside and replaced me so they could get co-financing from another major. I never felt so sold out in all my life. I fought right up to the time they fired me." Lumet eventually brought *Prince of the City* to the screen in 1981 with Treat Williams in the lead.

Determined to steer clear of the horror genre, De Palma returned to his old Alma Mater, Sarah Lawrence College, and taught a film-school class. He also put together a movie project based on one of his old unfilmed screenplays—a semi-autobiographical story about a student who becomes obsessed with catching and filming his father in an adulterous act—that his students rewrote and then co-directed with him as an independent feature. The result was *Home Movies*, an attempt to return to the looser, improvisatory feel of his early comedies like *Greetings* and *Hi Mom!* De Palma gave the lead role to newcomer Keith Gordon and filled up the rest of the cast by calling in favors from actors he had worked with in the past such as Gerrit Graham and Mary Davenport, the mother of Jennifer Salt. Kirk Douglas also agreed to appear in the film and offered to stump up part of the budget. *Home Movies* might well have been a noble experiment, but it was a complete disaster at the box office.

There were other disappointments. De Palma had been interested in making a movie of author Gerald Walker's 1970 novel *Cruising*, about a cop chasing a psychopathic killer through the gay underworld, and had even worked up a script for the proposed film. But he couldn't secure the rights to the novel and had to abandon the project. Instead, *Cruising* was picked up by director William Friedkin, who cast Al Pacino in the lead.

De Palma may well have breathed a sigh of relief at having made a narrow escape when Friedkin and Pacino found themselves at the center of angry protests by the gay community over the portrayal of the homosexual lifestyle in *Cruising*, but he was about to become the target of an intensive hate campaign himself.

Having dodged one bullet, he walked straight into another one.

8

"Make way for the bad guy."

Tony Montana

As the 1970s drew to a close, De Palma revisited territory he had already explored with *Sisters* back at the start of the decade.

The film was *Dressed To Kill*.

Dressed To Kill had been partially rescued from the bones of De Palma's *Cruising* script. Unlike William Friedkin's version of *Cruising*, De Palma's take on the story fleshed out the character of the killer by making him a third-rate actor and, in a nod to Michael Powell's classic psycho-sexual study *Peeping Tom* (1959), having him film all of his murders. One of these murders is of a sexually frustrated housewife who has a brief sexual encounter, only to discover that she may have contracted a sexually transmitted disease. This episode became the springboard for the new script.

Dressed To Kill modeled itself on *Psycho* not only through its central premise of a transvestite killer punishing "wicked" women, but also by following Hitchcock's lead of unexpectedly dispensing with his apparent leading lady, here played by Angie Dickinson as the sexually frustrated housewife, early on in the film. The plot then changes direction and focuses on Nancy Allen, who plays a prostitute who has witnessed the murder and becomes the killer's next target. Keith Gordon from *Home Movies* was here cast as another nerdy teenager, the son of the murdered housewife, whom Allen enlists to help her catch the killer. And so as not to leave anyone in any doubt as to the inspiration behind the movie, De Palma threw in not one but two shock shower scenes.

However derivative, *Dressed To Kill* was a slick, glossy horror thriller and proved to be a major box-office hit in the summer of 1980. The critics were divided over the movie. The *New York Times* called it "a witty, romantic psychological horror film" and leading critic David Denby proclaimed it "the first great American movie of the '80s". Other reviewers felt that De Palma's fascination with Hitchcock was beginning to grow stale and that the director was all style and no substance. As a headline in *Rolling Stone* magazine put it: 'Brian De Palma: The New Hitchcock or Just Another Rip-off?'

De Palma shrugged off the comparisons to Hitchcock, even admitting "The fact is I don't wholly admire Hitch. There are a lot of things I actually don't like about him at all —like his last few films, for instance. I don't like the way he views people, as if he doesn't really like them much."

He said that comparisons were inevitable given the type of films he was making. "Hitchcock made 50 movies and explored every kind of visual grammar of suspense and action. So somewhere, if you're working with this type of visual storytelling, you're going to be using material Hitchcock has used before. You have somebody walking down a corridor or going up a flight of stairs—he's used that shot somewhere before. It's impossible not to fall into his grammar, which is, of course, the best." He himself likened

Dressed To Kill to Luis Buñuel's *Belle de Jour*, saying the movie was about "a woman's secret erotic life".

But snide remarks about his debt to Hitchcock were the least of De Palma's problems.

By far the most vociferous criticism of the movie came from feminists. Groups such as Women Against Violence Against Women (WAVAW) were outraged by *Dressed To Kill* and decried it as pornography, arranging protests outside theaters screening the film and attacking it in the press. "WAVAW does not advocate censorship," stated a spokesperson. "We're only asking for responsibility... What people see on the movie screen is more than art. Its messages influence society." However, some more militant groups of feminists went further, invading screenings of the film and splattering red paint on the screen.

Having earlier engaged in an angry battle with the censors over *Dressed To Kill* and reluctantly cut his film, De Palma was once again forced on the defensive. Of the notion that his film encouraged violence towards women he had this to say: "If you have a misogynist outlook a sexist film could strike a chord in you, but I don't think it engenders sexism. I don't think women are beaten or raped because the rapist has been affected by the entertainment industry. If there were statistics to prove that, they'd be on the front page of every newspaper in the country."

As for the violence directed at both Angie Dickinson and Nancy Allen in the movie, he argued, "Women in peril are inherently more dramatic than men in peril, because they're more vulnerable. It's just a convention of the genre. But now, if you put a woman in peril, you're into a political issue of violence against women, when you're just thinking about making an effective horror movie. I think it's unfair. If a man gets killed, does that make it any better or more morally redeemable?" He defended the brutal razor murder of Angie Dickinson in aesthetic terms: "I read somewhere that the most terrifying thing for a woman is disfigurement, that disfigurement is worse than death—that a woman would rather be stabbed than have her face cut up. It seemed to me a particularly terrifying image."

Angie Dickinson supported De Palma against his feminist critics: "These people want all movies to be Walt Disney. We should want movies to show the complexities of our consciousness. *Dressed To Kill* is down-to-earth honest."

Nevertheless, De Palma was branded a misogynist and the label stuck. It was pointless to point out that the director had treated even the most dysfunctional of female characters with an enormous amount of sympathy in films such as *Sisters, Carrie* and *The Fury*. And while much was made of the fact that he had cast his own wife as a prostitute in *Dressed To Kill*, she wasn't simply a two-dimensional victim but a character of depth and resourcefulness. If anything, it was the male characters in De Palma's films that invariably came across as weak, misguided and ineffectual.

Even while he was struggling to defend *Dressed To Kill*, De Palma was rushing into his next movie, tentatively entitled *Personal Effects*. However badly it might have been maligned in the press, *Dressed To Kill* had made a lot of money at the box office. Filmways Pictures, the independent company that had backed the film, were more than happy to bankroll De Palma's next project. Although Filmways had been in existence since 1960, its merger with American International Pictures in 1979 had given the company new impetus.

The screenplay for *Personal Effects* had had a curious genesis. Back in 1979, De Palma and the Canadian film journal *Take One* had come up with a competition designed to give first-time writers a break in the movie business. De Palma supplied the outline—a political thriller based in Montreal about a man who accidentally overhears an assassination attempt—and got writers to use it as the basis for an original screenplay, with a view to De Palma filming the winning entry.

In the end, *Take One* magazine folded, the winning screenplay was shelved and De Palma fleshed out the story himself. It revolved around a movie sound effects engineer who, whilst out one night making recordings in the country, witnesses a car crashing into a river. The accident results in the death of a presidential candidate and, after listening back to his recordings, the engineer realizes the car had been forced off the road by a gunshot, from which point he begins to unravel a complex political conspiracy. The title was eventually changed to *Blow Out*, an homage to Michelangelo Antonioni's *Blow Up* in which a photographer (David Hemmings) suspects he has inadvertently taken a photo of a murder.

Although De Palma had envisioned either Richard Dreyfuss or Al Pacino in the role of Jack Terry the sound engineer, John Travolta expressed enthusiasm for the part after reading the script. De Palma had been wary of casting his wife Nancy Allen in the main female role, a good time girl Jack rescues from the submerged car after the accident, partly because they hadn't wanted to work together again so soon after *Dressed To Kill* and partly because of snide comments that he seemed to repeatedly cast Allen as a prostitute (as well as *Dressed To Kill*, Allen had also played a hooker in *Home Movies*). Allen only got the role because Travolta, with whom she had enjoyed great on-screen rapport in *Carrie*, cajoled De Palma into giving it to her.

It's hard not to read the opening of *Blow Out* as an attempt by De Palma to bid farewell, once and for all, to horror movies. The movie begins with a lengthy pastiche of slasher movies as a psychotic killer stalks a nubile young woman. As the killer advances on the girl, she stares at him in horror and a pitiful squeak emerges from her mouth. At that point, the viewer becomes aware that they are watching a film-within-a-film and that Jack Terry is in the process of dubbing the soundtrack of this cheesy B-movie. In an ironic twist at the end of the picture, Jack finds the perfect scream to put in the mouth of the starlet by using Allen's real-life death shriek after he had been unable to save her from being murdered by the political conspirators. The film closes on Jack's despairing face as he is forced to listen to Allen dying over and over and over again.

Blow Out was a dark, serious, and deeply pessimistic film, very much a throwback to such paranoid political thrillers as *The Parallax View* (1974) and *All the President's Men* (1976) in the mid-1970s. It was a film of real depth and power, not just dealing with De Palma's usual cinematic obsessions but engaging with the real world of the JFK assassination and the Chappaquiddick and Watergate scandals. Indeed, De Palma had been held rapt by the Watergate hearings just a decade earlier. Unfortunately, not everyone shared his interest.

Despite praise from certain quarters of the press—notably from *The New Yorker's* Pauline Kael, a longtime De Palma supporter and one of the most respected film critics in the world—*Blow Out* was met with mostly dismissive reviews. And word of mouth on the film was non-existent. It was an absolutely colossal flop at the box office.

To make matters worse, the film had come with a hefty price tag.

"*Blow Out* was always thought of as a very small movie... not particularly expensive because it was such a bizarre kind of idea," said De Palma. "Well, suddenly it became a big production with John Travolta, it went from an $8 million movie to an $18 million movie, and after the success of *Dressed To Kill* it was: 'Whatever De Palma wants to do, we'll let him loose!' So I went for it, and I'll never forget the first time the distribution companies saw the movie with that ending..."

The cost overruns on *Blow Out* had not been entirely De Palma's fault. While the film was in production, someone had stolen a truck loaded with 50 boxes of film. The missing reels contained all of the footage from the film's grand finale—an elaborate staging of a Liberty Day parade in the streets of Philadelphia—which meant the entire ending had to be reshot from scratch at a cost of almost $1 million. Even with insurance coverage, the theft created huge logistical problems for the cast and crew. The missing reels were never recovered.

Blow Out's box-office potential was also hampered by the fact that Filmways Pictures was on the verge of going into liquidation just as the film was being readied for release. This hard-to-sell film ended up being released with minimal marketing support, which pretty much drove the final nail into its coffin. Filmways was eventually absorbed into Orion Pictures, the very company which had sacked De Palma from *Prince of the City* just a few years earlier. Orion were to declare themselves bankrupt in 1992.

In the end, *Blow Out* scraped up just $9 million at the box office. If *Dressed To Kill* had been De Palma's biggest commercial hit to date, *Blow Out* was undoubtedly his biggest flop.

At the beginning of the 1980s, De Palma found himself in a very strange place.

He was exhausted from shooting *Dressed To Kill* and *Blow Out* virtually back to back. He felt under siege from the press, who had branded him a sadistic misogynist or worse, and his fans, who felt betrayed presumably because *Blow Out* had not been sadistic or misogynistic enough for their tastes. His only films that seemed to make money were horror movies, a genre he had grown to resent, if not despise. Any attempt to break into the mainstream was an unmitigated disaster. To put the final cap on the situation, all of the above had placed his marriage to Nancy Allen under pressure.

De Palma felt he was slipping farther and farther behind his friends and contemporaries, Steven Spielberg, George Lucas, Francis Ford Coppola, and Martin Scorsese. As George Litto, who had produced *Obsession*, *Dressed To Kill* and *Blow Out*, sympathized: "Brian never felt he was as successful as Marty, Francis, or George. That made him very uncomfortable."

De Palma tried to be philosophical about the situation. "That Brian De Palma is a powerful director is an illusion of Hollywood. Don't be sucked in by that. It's Tinseltown out here. Everything is sort of coated and unreal. When you make a movie like *Blow Out* and the movie makes 20 cents, you're verboten. Forget it. Despite Pauline Kael, despite anybody. You can't get a job. I have a certain corrosive vision of society which seems to not be very commercial. I try not to let my vision corrode the movies to the extent that they become so dark that nobody wants to see them. I did that in *Blow Out* and nobody really cared. The system goes on."

Yet if it was business as usual in Hollywood, De Palma was out of the loop. "No one would answer my phone calls after *Blow Out*," he sighed. "It was a very bad time."

Then, out of the blue, producer Martin Bregman came calling about a new version of *Scarface*.

And De Palma saw the light at the end of the tunnel.

9

"You wanna go with me, you say it.
You don't, then you make a move."

Tony Montana

Left to his own devices, the film Brian De Palma would have
chosen to direct after *Blow Out* was the complete antithesis
of *Scarface*.

For the director, *Blow Out* had been a first step towards
distancing himself from horror movies. "After *Dressed To Kill*, I
felt that I had pushed the horror/suspense genre as far as it
could go. To make another film like that, I would only be
repeating myself. I wanted to make a movie with real
characters which was set in a real situation instead of the
Brian De Palma world—one step removed from life where I
had been working."

For a short while, De Palma had become interested in
working on one of John Travolta's pet projects, a biopic of
Howard Hughes simply entitled *Mr Hughes*. He had also
written another screenplay, a musical drama entitled *Fire*, for
Travolta, which would have cast the actor as a doomed rock
singer loosely based on Jim Morrison of The Doors. (This
wasn't as strange a project for the director as it might sound;
De Palma had always been a big rock 'n' roll fan. Back in the
mid-1960s, just after he had finished making *The Wedding
Party*, De Palma had embarked on a music documentary

entitled *Mod* and had traveled to London to film a number of rock bands, including The Who and the Rolling Stones, performing in concert. Eventually, he ran out of money and was forced to abandon the project, indefinitely shelving the footage he had already shot. And immediately after making *Scarface*, De Palma filmed the promo video to accompany the Bruce Springsteen single "Dancing in the Dark"—a straightforward concert performance in which a then-unknown Courteney Cox is plucked from the audience to boogie with The Boss.)

However, there was one project that took precedence over either *Mr Hughes* or *Fire*.

De Palma had been hawking a screenplay entitled *Act of Vengeance* around the Hollywood studios, hoping that someone would bite. Despite its lurid title, the film was a sober political drama based on a non-fiction book written in 1974 by author Trevor Armbrister concerning union corruption in the American mining industry. De Palma had already written the script in collaboration with novelist Scott Spencer.

The story revolved around the slaying of Joseph Yablonski, his wife Margaret and daughter Charlotte in Pennsylvania in early 1970, when the family were discovered to have been gunned down in their own home in a brutal, cold-blooded mass murder. Yablonski had been active in the United Mine Workers of America for over three decades and was openly critical of the union's president, Tony Boyle, who had introduced a significant number of measures that had a detrimental effect on the lives of union members. In 1969, Yablonski directly challenged Boyle for the presidency and was found murdered just a few months later. Three killers were quickly found guilty of the slayings, but it took a further four years for Boyle to be charged officially with having sanctioned the assassinations.

As De Palma envisioned it, *Act of Vengeance* would have been a small, serious film more in line with the somber *Blow Out* than the lurid excesses of *Dressed To Kill*. But, as he observed bitterly, "it's been turned down 27 times because no one wants to make a film about the coal miners and their problems."

So when Bregman presented him with the *Scarface* project with Al Pacino already attached, De Palma jumped at it.

As he later told *Esquire* magazine, *Scarface* was going to be the film that would finally give him "dignity".

De Palma immediately began working on the screenplay of *Scarface* in collaboration with playwright David Rabe, with whom he had previously collaborated on the ill-fated *Prince of the City*.

Try as they might, however, they found it difficult to bring the screenplay into focus.

The initial concept was to try to remake the film as a period piece, a traditional gangster movie set in Chicago in the 1920s. However, De Palma had reservations about whether a large scale-period film could be made for the proposed budget of $18 million. The costs of dressing both the sets and the actors on such a film inevitably sent costs into the stratosphere. (Many years later, when De Palma actually got to make his lavish Chicago-set period movie, *The Untouchables*, the budget limited the choices he was allowed to make as a film-maker. The film was meant to have included a car chase through the streets of the city that had been scripted by De Palma and writer David Mamet but simply could not be achieved with the money available. Instead, De Palma transformed the scene into a confrontation in Chicago's Union Station, improvising and shooting the entire sequence in one night. It turned out to be probably the most memorable scene in the entire movie.)

De Palma and Rabe then explored the idea of updating the story to the present day. But they simply couldn't find a modern idiom that would encompass the rise and fall of an Italian gangster like Tony Camonte. The face of the Mafia and organized crime had changed irrevocably in the half-century since Al Capone had ruled Chicago with an iron fist wrapped in a velvet glove. From whichever direction they tried to approach the character, he remained an anachronism.

"The screenplay was not exactly going like everybody wanted it to," De Palma was forced to admit. "Ultimately, we couldn't agree on what we were trying to do."

Al Pacino sympathized with the director. "I remember that, for years, Martin Scorsese and Robert De Niro had a *Scarface* movie in their repertoire of things they wanted to do. But it was a difficult thing to break through and find a way to do in today's world."

Frustrated by his inability to crack the *Scarface* script, De Palma began to grow weary of the production. He was forced to confront the possibility that he had decided to become involved with the project for the wrong reasons. "There's a whole swirl of emotions that go into the decision," he once said. "A lot of times you make movies because you don't want to think about what's happening with the movie you just made. You don't want to think about the reviews out there or about how you're going to survive the pummeling that you're getting."

At the same time as he was confronting his misgivings, he discovered that someone over at Paramount Pictures had read the *Act of Vengeance* script and that they were interested in talking with him.

De Palma met with the Paramount executives and thought "My God, a miracle, we're going to make this movie."

So he resigned from *Scarface*.

Enthusiastic about a movie for the first time in months, De Palma waited to hear back from Paramount about *Act of Vengeance*. "I sit around. I get a call at my hotel; I'll never forget it. The executive says 'I want to say one word to you.' I'm expecting 'Go' or 'Congratulations.' And he said '*Flashdance*'."

Flashdance was a screenplay that had been kicking around at Paramount for some time and which they hoped would tap into the teen dance market in the same way as *Saturday Night Fever* and *Grease*. It was the unlikely story of a female steelworker who leads a double life as an exotic dancer in a seedy bar. However, Paramount were finding it difficult to line up a suitable director for the project. Their first choice, the British film-maker Adrian Lyne, had already passed on the film twice.

Against his better judgment and for all the wrong reasons, De Palma agreed to direct the film. "I knew it would make a lot of money and, naïve fool that I was, I believed the producer would consider my script on the Yablonski murders if I just made *Flashdance*."

He lasted just two weeks into filming before acknowledging that he had made a mistake and quitting the project.

For the time being, De Palma was left without a movie in the works.

10

"Never underestimate the other guy's greed."

Frank Lopez

When De Palma disentangled himself from the *Scarface* project and went off to make *Flashdance*, history repeated itself.

With Bregman casting round for a new director to helm his gangster epic, he approached the man whom everyone had assumed he would have approached in the first place: Sidney Lumet. It was pure coincidence that Lumet was the very director who had replaced De Palma on *Prince of the City* just a few years earlier. *Prince of the City* had eventually been released to theaters just a month after *Blow Out* but, despite very good reviews, was considered to have under-performed at the box office. This was to mark Lumet's third misfire in a row, following the flop pop musical *The Wiz* (1978) and the little-seen comedy *Just Tell Me What You Want* (1980). He wanted a cast-iron hit every bit as much as De Palma did and the notion of being reunited with his former collaborators on *Serpico* and *Dog Day Afternoon* must have held a lot of appeal.

Lumet was initially attracted to the idea of a *Scarface* remake. After giving it some thought, he came up with an inspired idea about how to update the movie and make it relevant to a modern-day audience. Lumet suggested setting the story in Miami and making the character of Tony

Camonte into a major player in the burgeoning cocaine trade. Turning to recent American history, he also suggested using the infamous Mariel boat-lift as the springboard for the story. Instead of being an Italian gangster, Tony could be a Cuban gangster.

Just a year earlier, in the spring of 1980, Mariel harbor in Cuba had become the focus of the American press. The repercussions of the events that began that year would reverberate through the United States long afterwards.

The crisis had begun almost unnoticed on April 4, when Fidel Castro, the Premier of Cuba, ordered that the armed guards around the gates of the Peruvian embassy in Havana be instructed to stand down. It was a provocative move for which Castro must have already anticipated the outcome. The Cuban economy was in a state of collapse, with the population struggling to survive despite shortages of jobs, food and medicine. A year earlier, the US President Carter had relaxed border controls between the two countries to allow Cubans and their relatives in America to visit each other. As a result, Cuban citizens had become painfully aware of the vast differences in social conditions between the countries and the vast opportunities that they felt were being denied to them. There had already been a number of violent incidents in Havana over the previous months, with Cubans mounting embassy invasions in an effort to seek political asylum.

With no guards in place around the Peruvian embassy, the building's grounds were immediately besieged by unhappy Cubans seeking asylum in Peru. Over the next few days, more than 10,000 refugees descended on the embassy, setting into motion a humanitarian crisis. Castro fanned the flames by refusing the Red Cross and other aid agencies permission to help the hordes camped out in the embassy grounds. Unwilling to become involved in the situation, US President Jimmy Carter issued this message: "Our hearts go out to the nearly 10,000 freedom-loving Cubans who entered a temporarily opened gate at the Peruvian Embassy just within the week." Privately, however, the US government was alarmed by this turn of events and what it might signify.

Fifteen years earlier, on September 28 1965, Castro had pulled a similar stunt by announcing that any Cubans wishing to leave the country were free to do so, effectively purging the country of dissidents who opposed his rule. The result of his decision had been the Camarioca boat-lift, in which refugees had fled the country for any destination prepared to accept them. The then US President Lyndon B Johnson had agreed to give sanctuary to the refugees and, since that date, a total of 665,043 Cubans had emigrated to America. It seemed as if history was about to repeat itself.

In an attempt to nip the problem in the bud and avoid another flood of immigrants, Carter agreed to impose a limit and only offer asylum for up to 3,500 refugees. Priority would be given to political prisoners, anyone seeking legitimate political asylum and Cuban citizens with families who had already settled in the US. Peru, Sweden and Belgium also agreed to accept a quota of refugees.

However, on April 15, Castro abruptly announced that he had opened the formerly closed port of Mariel to the world and that anyone wishing to leave Cuba would not be hindered. He also contacted the Cuban community in Florida and invited them to send boats to pick up refugees. Within a matter of days, any vessel that could be bought, borrowed or stolen had set out for Cuba. The Mariel boat-lift had begun.

The boat-lift was to become the US Coast Guard's single biggest operation in peacetime as thousands of boats, many of them unseaworthy, set out for Mariel harbor. It was only when the first flotilla had returned to Florida on April 21, that the authorities had begun to realize the magnitude of the situation. Wave upon wave of refugees were ferried to Miami, with many of the vessels then immediately returning to Cuba to collect another boatload. By May, the US Navy had been mobilized to help the Coast Guard to escort the vessels, along with 900 reservists called up to avert another humanitarian disaster.

Meanwhile, the US government was also struggling to process the overwhelming number of refugees arriving on American soil and was forced to create internment camps to hold the immigrants awaiting naturalization. Aware that the situation was getting out of hand, Carter ordered all boats to return from Mariel without any further refugees, but Castro refused to let the vessels leave the harbor unless they continued to lift people. It has also been alleged that Castro used the opportunity to empty his prisons and hospitals, secreting criminals, the mentally infirm, and the terminally ill amongst the genuine refugees. He was, it was claimed, attempting to purge the country of any undesirables and anyone who might cause a drain on Cuba's already threadbare social services.

The Mariel boat-lift officially came to an end on September 28, although Mariel harbor was to remain open for a further month and was only closed on October 31. By that time, more than 125,000 Cubans had made their way to the United States in what Jimmy Carter described as "a spontaneous and dramatic expression of their faith in freedom, of their desire to escape the oppressive Castro regime, and a desire to reunite long-separated families."

The extent to which hardened criminals numbered amongst the Cuban immigrants ferried to America during the Mariel boat-lift has always been open to question. Jimmy Carter admitted: "There is evidence that the Cuban government exported the undesirable elements to the United States in a calculated effort to support a propaganda contention that all of those Cubans who have come to the country are undesirable." However, there were many who also felt that the problem had been exaggerated by political opportunists in America in an effort to smear both the Castro regime and the perfectly legitimate immigrants who had arrived in the country.

Whilst there is little doubt that a certain number of the supposed refugees were indeed criminals, a conservative estimate was that they amounted to around less than two percent of the total boat-lift. Much was made of the fact that 23,000 immigrants held criminal convictions, although most of these were for petty crimes or for offences that were considered unwarranted in the United States, such as speaking out against the Castro regime or taking part in political demonstrations. In total, only 2,746 individuals were deemed to be actual undesirables and were denied American citizenship.

The concept of transforming the central character in *Scarface* into a Cuban criminal appealed greatly to Martin

Bregman. He had long envisioned the story as a metaphor for the American Dream, of the gangster as a businessman rather than a criminal. And who better to embody this idea than a disenfranchised opponent of Communism, who views his arrival in America as an opportunity to rise to the top of the capitalist heap?

Finally feeling that the *Scarface* project was coming into focus, Bregman also had the inspiration to bring a new creative partner on board.

A volatile young writer who could give the script the kick it needed.

And he already had a writer in mind.

man in the white suit: The original poster for the 1983 version of Scarface. *Director Brian De Palma was
...ed to intervene when the initial design concept depicted Al Pacino as Tony Montana in a black suit.*

Too hot to handle:
The original poster for
Howard Hughes and
Howard Hawks's
1932 version of
Scarface, which was
only released after a
year-long battle with
the US censors.

The public enemy:
Chicago mobster
Alphonse Capone,
who liked the 1932
version of Scarface so
much that he owned
his own personal print
of the film.

Gorilla at large:
Paul Muni as Tony
"Scarface" Camonte,
a performance that
director Howard
Hawks described as
"sub-human, ape-
like". That was a
compliment.

King of the underworld:
Al Pacino as Tony
Montana, a role which
screenwriter Oliver
Stone modelled in part
on Shakespeare's
Richard III.

Gangster No 1: Al Pacino's earlier foray into gangster movies, playing Michael Corleone in The Godfather ir

*Blonde Venus:
Michelle Pfeiffer as
Elvira Hancock, a
role she won despite
the objections of the
film's director
Brian De Palma.*

*Our man in Havana:
Steven Bauer as
Manny Rivera.
Bauer was the only
actual Cuban-born
member of the
Scarface cast.*

*Miami vice: Robert
Loggia as veteran
mobster Frank Lopez.
Loggia dyed his
naturally white hair
for the role.*

Three kings: Producer Martin Bregman (left) and executive producer Louis A. Stroller (center) confer with Br[i]
De Palma. They faced stiff opposition from Cuban pressure groups and the censors to bring Scarface *to the sc[reen].*

The big chill: Brian De Palma (left), Al Pacino, and Steven Bauer on the Scarface *set in LA. Although the c[ast]*
feigned basking in the Miami sun on camera, freak cold weather had everyone huddling in coats behind the sce[ne].

...gie nights: Tony Montana with Omar Suarez (F Murray Abraham, left) and Frank Lopez (Robert Loggia)
...be Babylon Club. The low camera avoided the reflections of the crew in the mirrored walls behind the actors.

...that money can buy: Manny and Tony relaxing in the master bathroom at the Coral Gables mansion.
...oduction designer Ferdinando Scarfiotti was given a free hand to dream up the most sumptuous sets imaginable.

A shot in the dark: Tony Montana and his "little friend" prepare for the final showdown at Coral Gables.

11

"You wanna play rough? Okay. Say hello to my little friend!"

Tony Montana

Just a few years earlier, Bregman had read a screenplay by a young aspiring film-maker named Oliver Stone, a semi-autobiographical account of his combat experiences in Vietnam entitled *The Platoon* (as with *The Star Wars*, *The Platoon* would later lose its definite article). Bregman was so impressed that he took out an option on the script and presented it to Columbia Pictures with a view to striking a deal to make the movie. The Columbia executives liked the script but were aware that Francis Ford Coppola was already working on his own Vietnam epic, *Apocalypse Now* (1979). Coppola had already earned a reputation as one of Hollywood's most visionary directors and had made a huge impression with his two *Godfather* epics. Columbia were wary of mounting a Vietnam War movie in direct competition with him.

Oliver Stone was also known to Al Pacino. The writer had penned no fewer than five screenplays about Vietnam. One of these, *Born on the Fourth of July*, had been specifically written with Pacino in mind to play the paraplegic Vietnam vet Ron Kovic. He and Pacino worked on the screenplay for over a year and came within a hair's breadth of making the movie. As Stone recounts: "We went through crew, casting, rehearsal —everything was done; we'd picked the locations and were set to start in six days when there was a hitch in the financing. It was co-financed by a German group, and they didn't come through. Then Al Pacino, who would've got an Academy Award for this one, got cold feet and walked away."

(Although Stone made those comments in 1981, his Academy Award prediction proved quite accurate; when he eventually completed *Born on the Fourth of July* with Tom Cruise in 1989, the actor did indeed get an Oscar nomination for his performance as Kovic.)

Columbia gave the thumbs down to *The Platoon*. By way of compensation, however, they introduced Stone to producer David Puttnam and director Alan Parker, who were then preparing a movie entitled *Midnight Express* (1978) and needed a writer for the project. The film was based on the memoirs of Billy Hayes, a young American who was caught attempting to smuggle drugs out of Turkey and thrown into a brutal Turkish jail.

Stone agreed to write the screenplay, but found it frustrating to work on a film in which he would have only partial creative control. "I always write as a director, as if I were shooting the scene frame-by-frame in my head. I've always seen through the camera. I've written several films for directors with a strongly defined visual style of their own, and sometimes they're better and sometimes they're worse than you imagined."

Although *Midnight Express* proved to be a hit and earned Stone both an Academy Award and a Writer's Guild award for Best Screenplay, the writer was tarnished by accusations of racism levelled at the film. He later observed: "I think that the racism in *Midnight Express* is a flaw in the film, but it doesn't spoil the whole. It was essentially a film about a miscarriage of justice. In the original screenplay there were more scenes with the Turks, and they were shown in a different light, with humor. However, Alan Parker, who is very visually creative and talented, doesn't have much of a sense of humor. So there was more humanity to begin with but then again, that would have made it a two-and-a-half hour movie. The film suffered because of it; the historical view is more narrow."

Stone had hoped that his work on *Midnight Express* would give him enough kudos to get a directorial assignment, but his subsequent Oscar proved to be something of a millstone round his neck. Instead of being perceived as a budding director, Stone noted ruefully "I became the next highly touted screenwriter."

Although Stone was of the same generation as De Palma, Spielberg, and Lucas, and had spent much of his youth absorbed by cinema, he'd arrived in Hollywood via another route entirely. Born in New York in 1946, the son of a Jewish-American stockbroker and a French mother, Stone spent most of his formative years in Europe, learning French before he could speak English. His love of the cinema was encouraged by his mother, who used to let him skip school in order to escort her to the movies. Particular touchstones in his cinematic awakening were Federico Fellini's *La Dolce Vita* (1960) and Roman Polanski's *Repulsion* (1965).

After such a privileged upbringing, Stone was devastated by the break-up of his parents' marriage in 1962. He dropped out of Yale in 1965, traveling to Saigon to teach English and subsequently joining the Merchant Marines. After more nomadic wanderings and a failed attempt to write a novel, he recklessly signed up for military service in 1967 and was sent on a 15-month tour of duty in Vietnam, earning the Purple Heart and Bronze Star for valor.

If his experiences in Vietnam were to give him the material for some of his most acclaimed movies, they also left another legacy. It was whilst patrolling the Cambodian border that Stone was introduced to drugs, specifically LSD and marijuana. Upon his return to the US, he spent two weeks in jail for trying to smuggle Vietnamese dope into the country.

Back in New York at the tail end of the 1960s, Stone confessed to being "pretty rootless and wanting to write." A friend suggested that he take up film studies at New York University and it was here that he met Martin Scorsese. As Stone noted: "He was so excited by the medium and he conveyed that enthusiasm to me." Stone began writing screenplays and directed several short films, eventually graduating in 1971.

The same year, Stone moved to Canada to make his first movie. It was a low budget horror flick entitled *Seizure* (subsequent releases of the movie sometimes bear the title *Queen of Evil*) which starred Jonathan Frid, a cult actor thanks to his portrayal of the vampire Barnabas Collins in the long-running daytime horror soap opera *Dark Shadows*. Frid plays a writer whose dreams are invaded by three monstrous manifestations of his own subconscious, a witch (Martine Beswick), a dwarf (Hervé Villechaize), and a giant (Henry Baker). The film was given a skimpy theatrical release and received a handful of good notices, but the distributors had only really invested in it as a tax shelter and it sank almost without trace.

It would be almost ten years before Stone would be handed another directorial project, coincidentally by the same producer, Edward R Pressman, who had helped Brian De Palma to make his breakthrough picture *Sisters*. It was another horror picture, entitled *The Hand*, based upon the novel *The Lizard's Tail* by Marc Brandel. In the meantime, he wrote screenplay after screenplay, many based on his experiences in Vietnam. But no one was interested in raking over the ashes of the Vietnam War at that time.

Pressman had originally approached Stone about directing *Conan the Barbarian* (1982), an epic fantasy based on the novels and stories of author Robert E Howard and to which he controlled the film rights. Stone wrote a script for the film, which he envisioned as a $40 million blockbuster to rival *Star Wars* and the beginning of a potential franchise. But studios were wary of entrusting such a colossal budget to a film-maker who had only one barely seen movie under his belt and, unable to secure a deal, Pressman sold on the rights to *Conan* to producer Dino de Laurentiis.

Stone's screenplay for *Conan the Barbarian* was passed on to director John Milius, but the pair had a falling out over Milius's rewrites. "Let's face it, John has a certain deafness— he doesn't listen," explained Stone. "There was no collaboration essentially. I wrote my stuff and I never really got a second pass. John rewrote, I gave notes, he tore up the notes, and then we never talked about the movie again."

In sheer frustration, Stone agreed to direct *The Hand* for Pressman. "Part of the reason I did *The Hand* was that it was obvious that studios weren't going to do the more dramatic material. So I thought, at least they'll do a horror movie for money. That's why I compromised, and I made a serious mistake."

Stone shot *The Hand* in 1980. The film bore some slight resemblance to *Seizure* in that its main character, played by Michael Caine, was an artist at odds with his own subconscious. Caine plays a comic book illustrator who loses his drawing hand in a traffic accident, after which he comes to believe he is being stalked by his own severed appendage, which has taken on a life of its own. Is he right in blaming the hand for a series of increasingly violent misadventures that occur around him, or is he himself responsible for his misfortunes, unknowingly venting his inner rage? In the film's near-nonsensical ending, Stone tries to have it both ways.

The Hand was a disaster at the box office. It was too arty to appeal to the average horror buff and too muddled to get more than polite nods from the mainstream critics. Because shooting the film had proved such an ordeal for Stone—he later admitted he had spent half of the shoot fighting with Michael Caine—he was left doubly demoralized by its failure.

12

"Is this it? Is this what it's all about, Manny?
Eating, drinking, fucking, sucking, snorting? Then what?"

Tony Montana

When Martin Bregman approached Oliver Stone about
writing the screenplay for *Scarface*, he was unaware that Stone
was on the verge of quitting Hollywood.

Stone was undergoing something of a personal crisis at
the time. Although he had met and recently married his
second wife, Elizabeth Cox, his personal life was otherwise a
mess. Ever since his combat experiences in Vietnam, Stone
had maintained a casual drug habit. But things had begun to
get out of hand: "After the war, I took it to excess. What I did
turned bad in the sense that it got heavier. My usage became
heavier, but not for a purpose. It became an indulgence."

To make matters worse, Stone had turned to the newest
recreational drug to hit America: cocaine. In the late 1970s
and early 1980s, cocaine had swept through America like a
blizzard. White powder was everywhere you turned,
especially among the fashionable movers and shakers in
Hollywood. As Stone's drug intake increased, it began to
seriously interfere with his thought processes and his
ability to work. "Cocaine is what took me to the edge. I
finally realized that coke had beaten me and I hadn't
beaten it."

Stone knew that he couldn't kick the habit if he stayed in America. He needed to go somewhere far from his regular suppliers and usual haunts, somewhere he wouldn't be tempted back into the cokehead lifestyle.

Thus at almost the precise moment Martin Bregman approached him to work with Sidney Lumet on the screenplay for *Scarface*, Stone had resolved to move to Paris.

By way of incentive, Bregman offered Stone $300,000 to stay on a little longer in the US to research the screenplay, after which he could move anywhere he liked while he wrote it.

Stone accepted.

The irony of asking a cocaine addict to write a screenplay that centered on the cocaine trade was not lost on Stone.

In truth, Stone had already done considerable research into drug trafficking for an aborted screenplay about the cocaine wars. He had got close to gangsters in Miami who were responsible for importing coke into the country, who had explained to him the circuitous route by which the shipments traveled from South and Central America to the Florida coast. He had even gone so far as to travel to Ecuador and Bolivia where he had partied with cocaine barons. The fact that he himself was cultivating a voracious drug habit helped get him access to important figures in the drug cartels, but hardly guaranteed his safety.

"I felt my life was on the line," Stone admitted. "Most of my work, for obvious reasons, was done between midnight and dawn. That's not the safest time to be out alone when you're dealing with people who might decide—on second thought—that they had told you too much.

"My wife was with me because she was like part of my security. A man with a woman seems a little less sinister or less intrusive than a single man. Naturally we struck up lots of conversations with guys with a lot of jewelry—playboy types—and I told them I was a screenwriter and I was doing a movie about this stuff. We started talking and went back to their place, drinking and snorting, having a party. Then I mentioned the name of somebody who had helped my research in Miami. This person had been a defence attorney. When I mentioned the name, their faces went white. It meant that I may have been connected in some way to the prosecution or to a cop or to an enforcement officer, and I was just pretending to be a screenwriter and was going underground here. I knew I was in trouble.

"It was a scary moment and it was good for me to get back in touch with the fear that I had felt so often in Vietnam. Because that fear is the essence of what *Scarface* is about. Those moments of fear and the concept of not knowing what's going to happen next, that violence can come at any time." Stone manages to capture much of that tripwire tension in the scenes in *Scarface* set in Bolivia, where a brief word in the right ear can result in an instantaneous death warrant being issued.

Having accepted the challenge of writing *Scarface*, Stone realized that he was going to have to research the subject in even greater depth. "I went to Miami extensively. I got to know both sides of the story. I got to know the law enforcement side, through the Attorney General's office. I got to know the gangster element, through the lawyers and ex-gangsters. Then eventually I wanted more and I plunged on into the Caribbean; I went down to Bimini." At the time, the island of Bimini in the Bahamas was a crucial link in the drug chain that stretched from South America to Florida.

Although Stone went out of his way to make friends in the Cuban community and acknowledged that they were frequently misrepresented in the press and the media, he was also wary of certain elements within the community. "The Cuban right wing is a very scary group. Honestly, even to talk about them is dangerous; they may be the single most dangerous group of guys I have ever met... It's the whole group from the Bay of Pigs. A few of them are drug dealers and use drug moneys to keep their political work going. A lot of these guys have disguised drug dealing as legitimate anti-Castro political activities, and that is mentioned in the movie."

In Florida, Stone spent much of his time hanging around with law enforcement officers from the City of Miami and Fort Lauderdale police departments, as well as the Dade and Broward County Sheriff's Department, talking to working cops and federal agents about their day-to-day experiences and delving into their files of case histories. Many of the events later fictionalized in his screenplay were based on events in the files, including the notorious chainsaw murder scene. "When I was in Miami, there were something like two hundred drug-related murders that year—and, in fact, there were two Colombians who were killed by chainsaws and carved up worse than in the movie."

Yet beyond all the grisly statistics, Stone began to detect a theme emerging from the research material that not only struck a chord in his imagination, but also reinforced Bregman's original feelings about the film. This was not just a tale about the rise and fall of an American gangster, but the rise and fall of an American businessman. As Stone said: "There was a fascinating theme there of immigrant growth; a kid with two cents in his pocket arrives on the shores of Florida and within two years is a kingpin making $100 million or $200 million a year. Where else in the world...?"

Stone remained in America just long enough to complete his research for *Scarface*.

Then he decamped to Paris for six months and went cold turkey.

Having researched the movie stoned, he wrote the screenplay "totally straight."

From the very start, Stone had a clear concept of precisely how he wanted his *Scarface* to play: "I always thought it was a comedic *Richard III*."

First performed circa 1594, Shakespeare's historical tragedy of *Richard III* charts the ruinous rise and fall of the deformed Richard, Duke of Gloucester. Ambitious to ascend to the throne of England, Richard conspires with the Duke of Buckingham to eliminate any rivals for the crown. This unquenchable thirst for power includes cold-bloodedly putting his two young nephews to death and marrying his own niece. However, Richard finds his hold on power is slippery, especially when the alienated Buckingham shifts his allegiance to the Earl of Richmond, who has been prophesied to one day become king himself. Buckingham and Richmond raise armies to overthrow the crown and Richard finds himself increasingly isolated. He meets his death at the Battle of Bosworth, cut down by

Richmond, who then ascends to the throne as Henry VII and establishes the Tudor dynasty.

With his twisted spine acting as a hideous metaphor for his warped sense of morality, Richard plots his ascendancy to the throne of England with exactly the same ruthless precision and lethal effect as Tony Camonte seizing control of the Chicago mobs in the original novel and film of *Scarface*. Yet within his quest for power at all costs lie also the seeds of his own destruction. Stone took these basic themes and then amplified them, structuring his new screenplay as a grand tragedy or, as Martin Bregman had described it, a "gangster opera".

He even began jokingly referring to it as *Scarfucci*.

Retaining the bare bones of the Ben Hecht screenplay for the 1932 version of *Scarface*, Stone expanded certain elements and reduced others. Tony Camonte became Tony Montana (the name was an homage to one of Stone's American footballing heroes, the quarterback Joe Montana), a violent thug sprung from jail in Cuba and transported to America as part of the Mariel boat-lift. Guino Rinaldo became Manolo 'Manny' Rivera, Tony's best friend since their days of military service in Cuba and a would-be ladies' man. Johnny Lovo became Frank Lopez, a cautious Cuban mobster already well established in Miami, who is at first impressed by Montana's ambition and bravado only to become alarmed by his ruthlessness and, eventually, another casualty in his inexorable rise to power. And the brassy gangster's moll Poppy became Elvira Hancock, the ice-blonde trophy mistress of Lopez, who uses cocaine to stave off her boredom and becomes the object of Montana's lust.

Stone also made explicit what Hawks and Hecht had only dared to hint at in their film, that Tony harbors incestuous longings for his sister. In Stone's version of the story, Tony is reunited with his kid sister Gina when he arrives in America. Gina Montana is an innocent Cuban hairdresser who gradually gets sucked into the glittering but corrupt Miami underworld and falls in love with Manny Rivera. As in the original novel and movie, Tony brutally guns down Manny when he finds him and Gina together, only to be informed that they had secretly been married.

Although the rise of Tony Montana broadly mirrors the rise of Tony Camonte, Stone was dissatisfied with the mobster's eventual downfall in the original movie. He wanted Tony Montana's downfall to mirror the reality of life in America. As he said: "The American Dream as we know it is founded on success, a sense of money and power. But most Americans fail; 99 percent of them are losers."

So he extended the story's final act, showing Montana becoming increasingly reckless as his dependence on cocaine worsens. He foolishly gets nabbed in a money-laundering scam and the only way he can avoid a prison sentence is by agreeing to assassinate the diplomat Orlando Gutierrez (a character based in part on Orlando Letelier, a former Chilean politician) who is planning to expose one of his business partners, the powerful Bolivian cocaine baron Alejandro Sosa. When he aborts the murder attempt in an abrupt display of conscience, Sosa swiftly despatches his private army to get revenge.

"I think it was more interesting to let Tony Montana destroy himself, to bring himself down," Stone explained.

"This seems to be the case if you study the history and the profiles of the drug lords. You see a pattern: money and excess and wealth. Luxury corrupts far more ruthlessly than war.

"Tony 'gets' the American Dream, but it's hollow because there's nothing going on spiritually. He can't love. He can't love Elvira Hancock. He can't reach out to her; he can't connect. All he can love is his sister. His blood. But his ability to imagine a form of love outside himself is impossible because of the materialism around him. It's destroyed by it. I thought it would be a great ending for him to be buried in a mound of gold dust or cocaine, just crash into it."

To a certain extent, Stone got a cathartic kick out of having Montana dive head-first into the mountain of white powder on his desk. He had always intended the script to be, as he described it, his "farewell to cocaine".

As he explains it: "I really wrote it off in a big way. What better farewell than a guy falling into a ton of cocaine, and when he looks up at the camera there is all this white powder up his nose. I think it's very funny."

Stone returned to Hollywood with the completed *Scarface* screenplay.

Martin Bregman loved it.

Al Pacino loved it.

Sidney Lumet hated it.

13

"Now you're talking to me, baby!
That I like! Keep it coming!"

Tony Montana

Oliver Stone was crushed when he discovered Sidney Lumet had rejected his screenplay.

"Sidney thought it was too violent and over the top," he said. "It wasn't what he wanted to do."

In an effort to steer the screenplay back into calmer waters, Lumet suggested introducing a sub-plot that would suggest that the CIA had become involved in the cocaine trade in an attempt to undermine Castro's communist regime. Martin Bregman thought Lumet's suggestions were counter-productive: "He felt the script should take more of a political direction. I felt that it not only wouldn't work, but that it wasn't true."

Bregman was more than satisfied with Stone's screenplay as it stood. "I think the direction we chose was pretty much embodied in the original *Scarface*, the elements that were basic in the construction of that film. Oliver, being the brilliant writer he is, invented the rest of it."

He was particularly impressed with the way that Stone had depicted the character of Tony Montana. "He was a dynamic character, he was an exciting character, he was a romantic character. He was all the things a movie gangster should be."

Similarly, Pacino was reluctant to abandon the new screenplay. "On the first reading of that script, I realized how Oliver had captured that world and made it his own, and brought out that wonderful texture and nuance and power."

Pacino had long been fascinated by *Richard III*—he had already appeared in the lead role in two major productions of the stage play, in Boston in 1972 and in New York in 1979, and would later write and direct a documentary, *Looking for Richard* (1996), which explored William Shakespeare's relevance in the modern world and couldn't have failed to detect the echoes of the character in Tony Montana. "The part of Tony Montana... was a chance to play someone absolutely fearless," he enthused. "He was like a meteor flying in the face of his own destruction."

Now at odds with both his producer and star, Lumet had little option but to gracefully bow out of the production, leaving the film rudderless once again.

Anxious not to lose impetus on the production, Bregman decided to take a chance and show Oliver Stone's new *Scarface* screenplay to Brian De Palma.

It might not have been the movie Sidney Lumet wanted to make but it was certainly the movie that De Palma wanted to make. As he put it: "Think about it: Cubans! Cocaine! Al Pacino! Machine guns! Girls! Wow! That's what I want to see."

"De Palma saw the film as I saw it," said Bregman, "and as Oliver had written it."

Having already tried and failed to come up with a workable *Scarface* screenplay, De Palma was fascinated by Stone's take on the story. "It was nothing I had ever envisioned and that was why I liked it so much. It was a whole new way of approaching this material.

"I liked the material specifically because it was a modern metaphor for *The Treasure of the Sierra Madre* where gold becomes cocaine. It's the American Dream gone crazy, where you have this product which you can turn into millions of dollars but, in the process, you destroy your life. It's the capitalist ideal gone bizarre and berserk and completely self-destructive."

(In fact, De Palma did film an early scene in *Scarface* where Tony and Manny watch a scratchy 16mm print of Humphrey Bogart in *The Treasure of the Sierra Madre* (1948) while still being held in the Freedomtown internment camp. Returning to their dormitory afterwards, they discuss the film:

Tony: "That Bogart, huh, chico..."

Manny: "He's fuckin' crazy, man! Shit!"

Tony: "All that gold dust blowin' in the wind... You see, Manny? He's always lookin' over his shoulder. Like me. Don't trust nobody, man."

Manny: "Man, I guess all that gold can make you so fucking crazy that you don't trust nobody no more."

Tony: "Never happen to me, chico. I'll never, never be crazy like that."

Manny: "Oh no? How d'you know this, eh?"

Tony: "Because I know."

Manny: "Oh yeah? I think you're a little crazy already, you know."

Ultimately, the scene was cut from the movie.)

Although he became enthused immediately by the challenges presented by Stone's script, De Palma also had certain misgivings: "I knew nothing about the Cuban cocaine trade at all. I knew nothing about dealing in an epic dramatic movie with all kinds of elaborate, exotic character types.

Scarface is basically about the relationship of a series of characters over a period of time, a saga, and I had never made a movie like that in my career."

Bregman and Pacino, however, were convinced he was the man for the job. Pacino said "I felt good when he was involved because, first of all, he responded to the script in such a passionate and positive way. This idea he had of making this thing larger than life, a little bit more heightened reality, appealed to me."

Later, De Palma returned the compliment when he admitted that, for him, "the most defining experience on *Scarface* was the opportunity to work with a truly great actor. It makes you better to work with a great actor because you've got to be driven to find ways to deal with the input they give you."

14

"In this country, you gotta make the money first.
Then when you make the money, you get the power.
Then when you get the power, then you get the women."

Tony Montana

There was one thing that was still bugging De Palma about
Scarface.

Having accepted the directorial assignment and plunged
headlong into pre-production on the movie, he still had
reservations about the budget.

After the problems encountered on *Blow Out*, he was wary
of starting a new movie already knowing that the budget
couldn't cover costs. De Palma had already seen how the
budget overruns incurred on *Apocalypse Now* (1979) and *One
from the Heart* (1982) had affected his friend Francis Ford
Coppola's standing in Hollywood. Coppola had gone
enormously over budget on both movies and left himself
heavily in debt; despite his reputation as a genius film-maker,
he had found that most Hollywood executives were wary of
bankrolling his movies unless they could put him on a very
tight leash. De Palma cherished his freedom and wanted to
avoid being lumbered with the restrictive reputation of being
a reckless and profligate film-maker.

Scarface had been greenlit by Universal Pictures at a
budget of $18 million (which, taking into account inflation,

would translate into a budget of approximately $34 million by 2004 standards). De Palma and his agent, Marty Bauer, were adamant it couldn't be brought in for less than $22 million and that $25 million (or $50 million by 2004 standards) would probably be closer to the eventual total. Perhaps wary of De Palma after the costly overruns of *Blow Out*, Universal eventually were convinced to increase the budget by a more modest sum to $23 million. (Perhaps unsurprisingly, the film ended up costing $25 million, precisely as De Palma and Bauer had predicted.)

Not being faced with the problem of having to search for a leading man, Bregman and De Palma set about assembling the supporting cast and the crew, holding auditions on the east coast. It was to be, in De Palma's words, "a long, arduous casting process."

Having had a certain amount of autonomy over the casting of most of his earlier movies, the director was suddenly faced with having to work closely with a producer who would have the ultimate say over who was or was not hired. Al Pacino had also reached the stage in his career where he could play a part in the decision-making process over the casting of supporting roles, to pick and choose precisely who he would be appearing with on screen. Thus whereas De Palma thought that John Travolta would be perfect to pay Manolo Rivera and put his name forward for the role, Bregman and Pacino insisted upon hiring the actor Steven Bauer instead.

Bauer was a young actor who had only previously appeared on television, but had sufficiently impressed the casting agent for *Scarface* to be brought to De Palma and

Bregman's attention. It is likely that Bauer's background weighed heavily in his favor. He had been born Esteban Echevarria in Havana in 1956, on the exact day that Fidel Castro had arrived in Cuba from Mexico to begin the revolution that would overthrow the Batista regime. The Echevarria family had fled the country when Esteban was four years old and relocated to Miami. He had first-hand knowledge of the whole immigrant experience.

Even though it was still early in the casting process, Bregman felt strongly that he wanted Bauer in the movie and said so at their first meeting. "Bregman, from day one, says 'Kid, you're gonna do this movie. You're gonna play Manny'," said Bauer, who was advised to sit tight and prepare until the rest of the cast could be assembled. Bauer was to be the only member of the principal *Scarface* cast who was an actual Cuban.

Pacino hit it off with Bauer straight away. "Steven and I became very close friends and spent much, much time together, just going over our relationship and what it had been in the past. We had fun doing that."

The rest of the supporting cast were selected through auditions.

The veteran actor Robert Loggia was cast as the aging Cuban mobster Frank Lopez. Loggia had begun his acting career in the 1950s by making a stab at establishing himself as a leading man in the cinema and on television. Yet if his craggy face and gravely voice had made him an often unconvincing screen star or matinee idol, they were just right for the colorful character roles to which he naturally gravitated. He became a very familiar face through regular appearances in numerous notable television series such as *The*

Wild Wild West, Cannon, Kojak, and *Starsky and Hutch* during the 1960s and 1970s. Whilst he excelled in roles as tough cops and steely mobsters, he also had a fatherly quality that could be called upon for gentler roles. It made him a good match for Lopez in *Scarface,* who had to display both the ruthless bravado of a successful career criminal, as well as a more open and benevolent nature that was to prove his downfall.

As Frank Lopez's venal and mistrusting right-hand man Omar Suarez, De Palma and Bregman cast the actor F Murray Abraham. Of Italian and Syrian origin but raised in America, Fahrid Murray Abraham was already something of a legend on the Broadway stage, although he had made only a handful of minor screen appearances in films such as *The Sunshine Boys* (1975), *All the President's Men* (1976), and *The Big Fix* (1978). He had worked with Al Pacino and Martin Bregman once before, in a very small supporting role as a cop in *Serpico.* Although De Palma would later describe Abraham as being "egotistical", he also found him a supremely professional actor with whom it was easy to collaborate.

Paul Shenar, who played the billionaire Bolivian drug baron Alejandro Sosa, was a more familiar face from television than the big screen, having appeared in the mini-series *Roots* (1977) and *Beulah Land* (1980). He had also starred as actor-director Orson Welles in the much lauded made-for-TV movie *The Night that Panicked America* (1975) about the Mercury Theater's infamous radio broadcast of H.G. Wells's *The War of the Worlds* that caused nationwide pandemonium in 1938. Shenar was an actor who excelled at oily villainy, which made him perfect for Sosa, and his rich voice had been used to great effect as the nasty rat Jenner in Don Bluth's classic animated adventure *The Secret of NIMH* (1982).

To play the corrupt cop Mel Bernstein, Bregman and De Palma selected another familiar face from 1970s television and cinema, actor Harris Yulin. The husband of actress Gwen Welles, Yulin had first caught the public's eye playing the lawman Wyatt Earp in the offbeat Western *Doc* (1971) and had subsequently starred in the cult fantasy adventure *The Legend of Hillbilly John* (1974), freely adapted from the stories of author Manly Wade Wellman, and the thrillers *The Midnight Man* (1974) and *Night Moves* (1975).

The only totally inexperienced screen actress was Mary Elizabeth Mastrantonio, who was to play Tony's sister Gina. Mastrantonio had performed on stage in New York, most notably in a revival of the musical *West Side Story*, but her only previous movie role had been as an extra in Martin Scorsese's *The King of Comedy* (1983), which had yet to be released. However, Mastrantonio had shone in her audition and had good chemistry with both Bauer and Al Pacino.

The only real concession to De Palma's usual repertoire of actors was an aural one. If you listen carefully during the opening interrogation of Tony Montana by the Immigration authorities, De Palma dubbed the voices of Dennis Franz, who had worked with the director on *The Fury*, *Dressed To Kill*, and *Blow Out*, and Charles Durning, who had appeared in *Hi, Mom!*, *Sisters*, and *The Fury*, into the mouths of the agents drilling him.

The hardest character to cast proved to be Elvira Hancock, the trophy mistress of Frank Lopez. De Palma and Bregman had considered virtually every young actress in Hollywood before eventually settling on Michelle Pfeiffer.

"There was a long process until we ultimately settled on the final cast," De Palma later said. "We were getting to the point where these decisions had to be made. Al would go back and forth, going 'Well, this is good, but this isn't quite working.' We ultimately had a screen test at the ninth hour and finally decided on Michelle."

It was a pretty big risk. Pfeiffer was a former teen model and beauty pageant winner from California who had not made much more than a gentle ripple with her early movie appearances in *Charlie Chan and the Curse of the Dragon Queen* (1981) and *Grease 2* (1982). De Palma had seen her in *Grease 2* —in which she played a member of the high-school clique the Pink Ladies—and wasn't impressed.

"When I went for the part," Pfeiffer admitted, "Brian De Palma actually refused to see me, saying he could never use 'that Pink disaster'."

However, she found a supporter in Martin Bregman.

"Michelle Pfeiffer was an actress that nobody had heard of," said Bregman. "Her agent called me and suggested that I meet with her. And I said that if she would be good enough to fly herself in (from California), I would see that she certainly would get a reading. And she did. For me, that was very important. I had every intention of paying for her transportation—which we did, a couple of months later—but if a young actor is that committed or that interested in doing a role that they would take their dollars—which are hard-earned dollars at that point in their careers—and make that kind of an effort to come in, we always pick up the tab."

For Pfeiffer, the audition was a trial by fire. She was asked to read opposite Pacino. "I was terrified, so terrified," she admitted. "I couldn't say two words to him. We were both really shy. We'd sit in a room, and it was like trying to pull teeth to try and find any words at all. And the subject matter was so dark. There was a coldness in the film relationship."

Bregman, however, witnessed something entirely different. "When she got up on stage in the theater that we used for casting, she brought Al to life. It's interesting because I don't think even he was aware of it. It happened. The relationship happened. It was right then and there. Nobody had heard of this girl, but she was just magic. There was no question in my mind, from the moment I saw her read, that she was going to do this part."

Pfeiffer turned out to be terrific in the role, if only because she brought considerably more to the part than had been present in the script. Oliver Stone had admitted that the character of Elvira as written by him was "the basic bimbo hanging round this Cuban gangster." Whilst Pfeiffer may not have had much in the way of dialog, she managed to transcend the limitations imposed by the script by suggesting layers of toughness and vulnerability.

As she said: "I was very excited to work with Al, but I was also intimidated by him. I had to play a cold and aloof woman, very different from my personality and a difficult character for me to hold on to."

Nor did Pacino make things easy for her during the lengthy *Scarface* shoot. The actor had studied under Lee Strasberg, the celebrated Artistic Director of the Actor's Studio in New York, and had become a devout believer in Strasberg's approach to method acting in which the actor allows themselves to become totally absorbed within a role.

Given their tempestuous relationship onscreen, Pacino insisted that he and Pfeiffer keep a certain emotional distance between themselves at all times. Which was not a comfortable way of working for an easygoing California girl who had undergone much less restrictive acting training. As Pfeiffer recounted: "I went through six months on the set with him looking at the ground whenever I was around."

Nevertheless, Pfeiffer impressed her more experienced co-star. "She was very attentive and committed," Pacino remembers. "She's a very involved working person. With this picture, I didn't know her and she wanted to discuss a lot about what was going on. I remember her being very intense and interested."

Despite Pfeiffer's earnest efforts to give the character some depth, Elvira remains the single weakest link in the movie. At no point is it adequately explained why such an obviously beautiful, intelligent, forthright person would be hanging around with a sleazy, aging mobster like Lopez, nor why she would simply acquiesce to Montana halfway through the movie. Compare her character to her counterpart in the Hawks/Hecht version of the story and there is world of difference between Poppy, the cunning, ambitious and sexually ruthless moll who dumps the ineffectual Johnny Lovo in favor of the dangerously potent Tony Camonte, and Elvira, the sleek, passive blonde simply being passed from hand to hand.

Similarly, Mary Elizabeth Mastrantonio found it difficult to transcend the limitations imposed on her by Oliver Stone's script. The writer simply wasn't very adept at writing fully three-dimensional female characters. Mastrantonio admitted:

"*Scarface* was heavy. I loved working with Al and Michelle very much. But it was an odd set to be on... I was shy and so was Michelle. It was a man's world and all these people with greasy hair and these big guns. We girls didn't know why we were there."

One girl who *wasn't* there was Nancy Allen, Brian De Palma's wife and the most conspicuous absentee from the *Scarface* casting sessions. Unknown to most people at the time, their marriage was on the rocks. It has been unkindly suggested in some forums that one of the causes of their disharmony was the fact that Allen had been passed over in favor of Pfeiffer for the role of Elvira, although she had never been seriously in contention for the part. De Palma dismissed the rumors: "I really don't know why two sensitive, intelligent people get divorced. I know I didn't marry to end this way. I had time in my life for her. I went home every night." Nevertheless, by the time *Scarface* was in theaters, the couple had separated.

With the entire cast in place, what followed was four solid weeks of rehearsals. Steven Bauer was amazed: "We had a month of rehearsal time! This is unheard of! Bregman insisted on it; Brian insisted on it. We rehearsed that thing to the point that we could have taken it on the road like a play!"

De Palma found the rehearsal time invaluable. He encouraged the cast to play around with their roles, to get into the skin of the characters, to feel at ease with their performances. He noted: "There was a lot of flying the scenes back and forth. Al and the other actors would improvise scenes and find things to build into the scenes. Then Oliver would come back and rewrite them."

Stone was to remain a presence on the *Scarface* set until the production wrapped. "When we came to shoot the film, Brian De Palma allowed me to take part in the film, to be there and study it," he explained.

Although De Palma later admitted that he had enjoyed a "lively collaboration" with Stone during the making of the film, his decision to allow him access to the set on a day-to-day basis would come back to haunt him much later in the production.

15

"I'm Tony Montana. You fuckin' with me, you fuckin' with the best."

Tony Montana

Although the character of Tony Montana was quite unlike any role that Al Pacino had played before on screen, he had had extensive experience of performing in villainous roles on stage in plays such as *Richard III* and *The Resistible Rise of Arturo Ui*.

Having initially been inspired by Paul Muni's performance in the 1932 version of the story, Pacino acknowledged that there were fundamental differences with the character Stone had created: "I think that this Scarface was a combination of so many different gangsters we've seen. He was representative of a collective person. He wasn't organized so much… he was a renegade. Even though he would comply, you knew that eventually he would never stick to any format, any controlled environment. He was out of control. Which was an attractive thing to play."

Unlike his previous foray into gangster cinema, playing Michael Corleone in *The Godfather* and its sequel *Godfather II* (1974), Pacino did not want to convey in Tony Montana the impression of still waters running deep. "When I started out to create this character, I pictured him in two dimensions, not three dimensions. This side and that side. This is what you see. I didn't try to go into another area with it."

Despite the monstrous activities with which Montana engages himself in the movie, Pacino refused to pigeonhole the character. "One doesn't see it as a monster," he explained. "You don't look at it like that. It's passions and emotion, and it's in all of us."

As to the character's perceived villainousness, he said "Well, it depends on what side of the street you're walking on... Anybody who says 'Go shove it!' when somebody's got a chainsaw that is about to take your head off—I think that is pretty much a hero in anybody's language."

To help Pacino develop his Cuban accent, Bregman turned to Robert Easton, the veteran dialog coach who had been dubbed 'The Henry Higgins of Hollywood' in honor of the George Bernard Shaw character who transformed Cockney flower girl Eliza Doolittle into an aristocrat in the play *Pygmalion*. Easton coached Pacino during rehearsal and throughout the production, giving him a number of catchphrases to help him master the intonation and pronunciation of the dialect. One of these phrases was "Look at these pelicans fly," which in Tony Montana's rolling patois became "Loog at dese Pelicangs flah." As an inside joke, Pacino actually uses this line in the scene where we see him reclining in his bubble bath watching a nature documentary on television. (It's also worth noting that he's actually looking at footage of flamingos, not pelicans.)

In addition to Easton, Bregman recruited a group of young Latinos to coach Pacino during shooting and offer advice on everything from accurate street lingo to physical gestures and mannerisms. "The group that we surrounded Pacino with in the film were basically all Cuban. Any time there was a problem with Al's accent, they had the right to interfere and suggest that he was off with it."

Pacino acknowledged a debt to these crewmembers in helping him nail Montana's character. "The Cuban people I met with and spoke with gave me a lot of insight into the mannerisms and suchlike. All of which I tried to put into a capsule, swallow and see what would come out. I was not trying to be authentic, because I don't believe you can really be authentic unless you can mimic very well." Instead, he tried to match his performance to the tone that De Palma was trying to capture, to "take the accent and the mannerisms, and just heighten them in a way for the movie, because Brian De Palma was going to take a larger-then-life approach to the film, to deal with the movie in an operatic style."

Despite the unrelenting grimness of the screenplay, Pacino tried to bring out the humor in Montana's character and succeeds in the more playful exchanges between him and Pfeiffer early in their relationship. As in the 1932 movie, a sort of childishness creeps into Montana's character in those scenes. "The humor was what I thought, right from the start, would be necessary. Because, if not, it was just going to be a one-way street. You needed to find those odd things, those twists, those ironies, to give the character some intelligence. Otherwise it would be too blunt, too hard to take."

In addition to his own preparations for the role, Pacino also made some unusual requests of his colleagues on the set. Director of photography John A Alonzo, who spoke fluent Spanish, remembers Pacino approaching him during rehearsals: "When I first met him, we were doing some screen tests, testing Michelle Pfeiffer. After we'd finished that day he said, 'Johnny, can I ask you a favor? Only speak Spanish to me when we start the movie.' I said, 'Really? Why?' He said, 'I want to *hear* Spanish. Maybe I won't understand, but just talk to me in Spanish.' So I did. For the entire picture, Al Pacino and I spoke Spanish. That's part of his preparation and I think that's part of what makes him one of America's finest actors."

Pacino's dedication to his performance, however, did take its toll on the actor as the production rolled on. The strain of maintaining the persona of such a malignant character was exhausting. "When I was in *Scarface*, I remember being in love at the time," the actor later admitted. "And I was so glad it was that time. I would come home and she would tell me about her life that day and all her problems. I remember saying to her 'Look, you really got me through this picture.' Because I would shed everything when I came home."

While Pacino worked on his accent and mannerisms, Brian De Palma was giving thought to the other essential quality of Tony Montana's physical embodiment: his scar.

"I was very worried that it would look phoney," he admitted. "That it was too big, that it was too small. So we did many make-up tests till we came up with something we all liked."

Pacino's input proved crucial in devising the final make-up design, which grew out of the elaborate back story he had constructed for Montana: "I felt this character was good with a knife and had fought with a knife. And the scar really came from one of those fights. I thought it would be interesting if it cut through the eyebrow and the action pulled my head away and it went down even further into the cheek. It was evocative of a chaotic wildness in this character."

As the film's pre-production phase came to an end, it seemed as if the film was progressing smoothly.

But the film-makers were about suffer a serious setback that was completely beyond their control.

16

"This town is like a great big pussy
just waitin' to get fucked."

Tony Montana

Martin Bregman and Brian De Palma had originally
envisioned *Scarface* as being shot almost entirely on location
in Miami, to take full advantage of the local color and
capture the vibe of the city.

Yet just before the project was ready to commence
shooting in September 1982, they were abruptly forced to
think again.

"We had scouted locations in Florida and were going to
shoot the movie in Florida," explained De Palma, "but then
the Cuban community became so outraged at how we were
representing them that they basically ran us out of town."

The Cuban community in Miami had begun to voice
concerns about a film which they claimed, wholly without
foundation, depicted all Cubans as criminals and drug dealers.

The spectre of *Midnight Express* raised its head again when
it was suggested that Oliver Stone was a racist. This was
particularly galling for Stone, who had done his utmost in the
Scarface screenplay to distance Tony Montana from law-
abiding Cuban immigrants. As Stone argued: "I think it's clear
that not all Cubans are drug dealers. The guy is—and his
mother even says he is—no good. It's classic gangster stuff.

But people get oversensitive, like when the Italians objected to Francis Coppola's doing *The Godfather*. It's like: 'We're not gangsters.' I mean, every nationality wants to believe there are no gangsters."

Some of the protests were even more misguided. As Bregman observed: "There were elements of the Cuban community that were convinced that this was a Castro-funded film, which was obviously not true. We were doing a gangster film! A theatrical film! An operatic theatrical film! But there were some people within the Cuban community—a small part of it—that were convinced we were out to hurt their reputation collectively."

De Palma and Al Pacino must have had a strong feeling of déjà vu. De Palma was still sensitive about the protests that had been conducted by Women Against Violence Against Women over *Dressed To Kill*, whilst Pacino had only recently had to weather the hostility mounted against *Cruising* by the gay community.

Bregman, however, was simply furious. "It angered me that nobody asked to see the script before they made judgments," he said, before adding "When they did ask, I told them to go to hell."

Stone was also reticent about handing over his screenplay. "A local newspaper even suggested in an editorial that, in its own interest, the Cuban community ought to have the right to look over the script—which would have been censorship."

When a number of personal threats were made to individual members of the cast and crew, Bregman decided the film couldn't continue under these conditions. "Making a movie is like mounting a military campaign. You want nothing suddenly coming from left field. Demonstrations, that's what worried me. How do you shoot a movie in a street with a demonstration in progress? It's hard enough to do it with everyone's cooperation."

Unable to placate the Cuban population, Bregman made the decision to abandon Florida and move the production to Los Angeles. The bulk of filming would take place in California, with a break to spend one week on location in New York City to film the attempted assassination of Gutierrez outside the United Nations building. The crew would only return to Miami for two weeks of location work right at the very end of the shooting schedule.

By which time, it was hoped, the fuss would have died down.

It was later estimated that the *Scarface* controversy cost the city of Miami somewhere in the region of $10 million in lost revenue when the film-makers left town. Ironically, former Miami City Commissioner Demetrio Perez Jr, a Cuban émigré who had spearheaded the protests against the film-makers and had suggested that the film sought to depict Cubans as criminals, was later accused of trying to sell his vote in the election of the new city manager in 1985, was arrested for trying to smuggle two handguns through a security checkpoint at Miami International Airport in 1999, and pleaded guilty to defrauding a government rent-subsidy program in 2001.

Relocating to Los Angeles set the *Scarface* production back several weeks and brought with it a new set of problems.

One of these was finding a location to match the Little Havana district of Miami, which was to have served as the colorful backdrop to Tony Montana's early career. Whatever location was chosen could not be recognizable as Los Angeles, so many scenes were rewritten to take place at night, when it would be easier to shroud familiar landmarks with darkness. In the end, the production team transformed the Little Tokyo district of LA into a replica of Little Havana, painstakingly removing all the signs featuring Japanese characters and replacing them with Spanish-language signage.

In some cases, however, the limitations that were placed on the crew worked to their advantage.

One of the most impressive shots in the film is the introduction to the Freedomtown internment camp, where the refugees from the Mariel boat-lift are incarcerated. Opening with a panoramic shot of concrete overpasses packed with traffic, the camera glides down to ground level, over the barbed wire fences and into the bustling thoroughfare of the camp. It is only then that we pick up the figure of Manny Rivera hustling his way through the crowds en route to meeting Tony Montana. The scene was vintage De Palma, an elegant crane shot seamlessly merging into a lengthy tracking shot, cleverly juxtaposing the gray, soulless concrete highways of the Land of the Free with the vibrant, carnivalesque atmosphere of the imprisoned Cuban community.

Yet as cinematographer John A Alonzo pointed out, that whole shot was actually forced upon the production team. The Freedomtown set had been built in the wasteland underneath the intersection of the Santa Monica and Harbor freeways. As a result, the positioning of the camera was dictated by natural landmarks. "If we had been levelled off," Alonzo admitted, "you would have seen that it was Los Angeles and not Miami."

The last scene to be shot on the Freedomtown set was the riot instigated by Tony and Manny to cover their assassination of the former Castro stooge Emilio Rebenga (Roberto Contreras). More than 600 extras, most of whom spoke little or no English, took part in the riot. The sequence was co-ordinated by the 40-strong stunt team, who coached the extras and then allowed them to literally demolish the set.

Since the *Scarface* budget could not accommodate any location shooting abroad—and since the feasibility of actually traveling to Bolivia to shoot the sequences in Alejandro Sosa's mountain stronghold would have been too dangerous to contemplate—the crew were forced to look closer to home to find a suitably imposing villa for the billionaire drug lord.

They found what they were looking for in the Californian town of Montecito in Santa Barbara, a few miles northwest of Los Angeles. Montecito was a small coastal settlement and the site of a former Spanish mission founded in 1769, which was blessed with rolling hills and natural hot springs. Since the early part of the 20th century it had become established as an exclusive holiday resort and many of Hollywood's wealthier citizens built houses there because of the privacy it afforded. These secluded hillside mansions provided a suitable alternative to rural Bolivia, and a handsome Spanish hacienda designed by the architect Addison Mizener was selected as the location for Sosa's private estate.

While touring Montecito, the location scouts also spotted a palatial mansion called El Fureidis (named after the Arabic word for 'paradise') a short distance away, and thought that this would be the ideal location for Tony Montana's Coral

Gables estate, the Xanadu-like fortress in which he incarcerates himself after his rise to infamy.

El Fureidis was a vast 35-acre estate that had been developed by the East Coast entrepreneur J Waldron Gillespie, who had spent years stocking the gardens with exotics plants and flowers. In 1906, Gillespie had commissioned architect Bertram Goodhue to design a Mediterranean villa inspired by Persian and European architecture. The estate had subsequently been the home of the writer Thomas Mann, and notable houseguests had included Albert Einstein and Winston Churchill. Silent comedy star Charlie Chaplin had married Oona O'Neill in the gardens of El Fureidis in 1943, which also served as the venue for the wedding of Tony and Elvira in *Scarface*.

Yet while the *Scarface* crew used all of their ingenuity to transform their LA locations into a plausible duplicate of Miami and Bolivia, even they had no control over the weather.

In the late autumn of 1982, the entire California coastline was wracked with unseasonable storms and the temperature began to plummet. As Steven Bauer noted: "On the radio they were talking about the threat to the orange crop. Meanwhile, we were shooting at night, dressed for the tropics."

A particularly ferocious storm also resulted in a sleepless night for the crew.

The set designers had already dressed the gardens of El Fureidis in preparation for the *Scarface* wedding sequence when Santa Barbara was hit by a momentous storm that was to cause over $1 million in damage throughout the county. Bregman and the rest of the production team were forced to sit out the storm in Los Angeles, anxiously awaiting reports from the location as to the extent of the havoc wreaked on the set. Luckily, the damage turned out to be minimal.

Another anxious moment for the *Scarface* crew was the day spent filming the death scene of Omar Suarez. In the film, Suarez is accused of being a police informer and then pushed from a helicopter with a rope round his neck by Alejandro Sosa's stooges.

Despite the fact that no one had ever attempted a stunt of this nature before, stuntman Richard Ziker agreed to go up in the chopper and do it "for real", while De Palma filmed him from below. Ziker had a special body harness built which would take the weight of the fall, rather than the noose round his neck. The stunt was completed without mishap and later intercut with close-ups of actor F Murray Abraham, who wore a similar harness to Ziker while simply being suspended from a crane above the studio backlot.

From the moment he had read Oliver Stone's screenplay, Brian De Palma had very clear ideas about the look of *Scarface*. "I wanted to do hi-tech, neon, acrylic, vibrant pastels instead of your usual dark film noir because you looked at South Florida and this was what it was all about. These guys dressed in white, not in black."

Director John A Alonzo, who had worked with De Palma before on the ill-fated *Get To Know Your Rabbit* over a decade earlier, was surprised by how much freedom he was given by the director. He was aware of the director's reputation for meticulously staged set pieces, for carefully planning and storyboarding every sequence. "I had expected Brian to give us these elaborate details of how he wanted the picture to look and what he wanted to work with. But all he said was, "John, I want you to give me the most beautiful pictures and I'm going to put violence inside.'"

Similarly, production designer Ferdinando Scarfiotti (who was not a union member and thus had to take the lesser credit of "visual consultant", despite being responsible for creating the elaborate set interiors on the soundstages at Universal Pictures) was given only the broadest instructions and left alone to allow his imagination to run riot. Scarfiotti had begun his film career collaborating with Bernardo Bertolucci on *The Conformist* (1970) and *Last Tango in Paris* (1972), but had more recently worked on Paul Schrader's *American Gigolo* (1980) and *Cat People* (1982) as well as Mike Hodges' 1980 remake of *Flash Gordon*. De Palma described him as "a genius."

Scarfiotti developed his design schemes to mirror Tony Montana's rise from "bleak and sordid" beginnings on the streets of Miami to the palatial mansion of Coral Gables in which he meets his untimely end. "As he moves up through the criminal hierarchy, the atmosphere becomes bright, brittle, glaring," Scarfiotti explained. "There is a sense of insane wealth. We are among people who amass such incredible sums of cash that they have to keep finding new ways to spend it. It goes on their walls, on the backs of their women, and into the playgrounds where they spend their lives."

The insanely opulent interiors dreamed up by Scarfiotti were exactly what De Palma wanted. As he explained: "I think it's important to establish that robbers enjoy the money they rob. They have a good time! The cocaine world is a crazy world. It's not just grim death and murder. It's fun! Clubs should be fun. The girls should be fun. There's a price to pay for all of this, but you have to show why they're there. They may be killers but they're kinda colorful."

Having been given freedom to indulge themselves, the technical and design crews occasionally found themselves working at cross purposes.

Alonzo remembers having a brief discussion with Scarfiotti about the set for the Babylon Club, which would be the location for one of the film's major set pieces, a chaotic gunfight that ensues after an attempt is made on Tony Montana's life.

Scarfiotti had designed a dazzling, cavernous interior for the nightclub, but only discussed the set with John Alonzo after it had already been built. As Alonzo recounts: "He asked me 'Do you mind mirrors?' I said 'No, I don't mind mirrors.' I figured there'd be one or two mirrors here or there. I walked on set and there's fifty panels of mirrors all the way around the walls! They gave us fantastic dimension, but made it almost impossible to shoot without catching the reflection of a camera or a technician. To add to the dilemma, Brian says 'I'd like to shoot two or three cameras.' That made it even funnier. So I had to check each camera to make sure the mirrors were not reflecting itself or the other cameras. And that when the mirrors were destroyed with gunshots that we weren't going to get an accidental reflection."

Although Scarfiotti did have the foresight to mount the mirror panels on pivots that would allow them to be minutely adjusted to take into account any awkward camera angles that might catch unwanted reflections, problems still arose. If you take a close look at the build-up to the gunfight in the Babylon Club, pausing on the final close-up of Tony

Montana slumped in his booth before the two gunmen open fire, you can see director Brian De Palma making an inadvertent (and one might almost say Hitchcockian) guest appearance reflected in the mirrors.

Scarfiotti's mirrors also caused a headache for the movie's special-effects team, who had to rig them to shatter once the gunfight commenced. Even though they would be shooting at the mirrors with plastic bullets, they were worried that flying glass would spray out and cut the actors and extras who would be milling around in the chaos. Initially they tried to resolve the problem by using plexiglass instead of glass, but the mirrors wouldn't shatter convincingly. Eventually, special-effects technicians Stan Parks and Ken Pepiot mounted the glass panels on a spongy backing known as Solitex and then covered them in a transparent film of plastic. "When we fired plastic pellets into the mirrors, the glass exploded without flying out," explained Pepiot.

Yet despite all the numerous problems the Babylon Club set posed for the film-makers, even Alonzo had to admit that it was "extraordinary."

If Alonzo admired the skill with which De Palma choreographed the film's set pieces, he was also impressed by how economical De Palma could be when he wanted. "Brian's ideas on the opening of *Scarface* were very interesting to me," he said. "They went against the grain, so to speak. Instead of using this big, wide crane shot to introduce the character, he introduces him in close-up, sitting in a chair, and he had the camera roll 360 degrees all the way around him. He did five or six takes like that and they were all close. I thought, 'What a fascinating thing.' In other words, he was introducing that face to the audience and the script is so good that you also felt the personality coming out, that arrogant behavior, that Latin machismo."

De Palma simply felt he was taking advantage of the film's greatest asset. "I think the most stunning thing about Al is his face," he explained. "He's the kind of guy who can hold the screen with his face. When you start a movie you want to give the lead character a very impressive entrance: that face, that character, that crazy shirt he's wearing, the scar, the way he moves, the way he talks. You just want to hit them with it, because you're hitting them with something they've never seen before. A lot of this had been reported on the news but no one had ever seen it in a movie before. These Cuban gangsters. The way they talked, the way they moved. Al embodied that in that close-up."

Although many critics had denigrated De Palma's directorial approach as being all style and no content, Alonzo didn't agree. "Brian likes to move the camera a lot, but he doesn't do it arbitrarily—what I call cinematic gymnastics. He does camera moves that are an integral part of the story."

However, there was at least one person on the set who disagreed with Alonzo.

17

"Nothing exceeds like excess."

Elvira Hancock

Oliver Stone had been present on the *Scarface* set for the entire shoot and wasn't entirely impressed with De Palma's working methods.

He was surprised by the length of time De Palma was taking to make the film and with the amount of effort he would lavish on each scene. Even knowing that he had written an 160-page script and that the finished film would run close to three hours (the accepted rule of thumb is that one page of script equals one minute of screen time), Stone felt De Palma was overshooting.

As he noted: "*Scarface* has a tempo that isn't the one I envisaged. If I'd made it, it would have had a more documentary style. With De Palma, one page of script became a minute and a half of film. He moves the camera more than I do, he's more 'operatic'. He made a four-hour film with an 160-page script so that he could cut it down to three hours in the end."

Mind you, Stone was probably also annoyed that, as the film ran over schedule, around 30 pages of his script ended up being junked simply because there wasn't time to shoot them.

One of those arbitrary cuts almost resulted in the loss of one of the film's most memorable moments. After the very public implosion of Tony and Elvira's marriage in a swanky restaurant, Elvira storms out and a hopelessly stoned Tony harangues the other diners with a brilliantly scripted soliloquy:

Tony: "What you looking at? You're all a bunch of fuckin' assholes. You know why? You don't have the guts to be what you wanna be. You need people like me. You need people like me so you can point your fuckin' fingers and say 'That's the bad guy.' So? What's that make you? Good? You're not good. You just know how to hide it. How to lie. Me? I don't have that problem. Me? I always tell the truth. Even when I lie. So say good night to the bad guy. Go on. It's the last time you're gonna see a bad guy like this, let me tell you. Make way for the bad guy. There's a bad guy coming through. Better get out of his way."

De Palma had already made his mind up that he was going to end the scene with Elvira's exit and Tony's dismissive response "Let her go. Let her go. Another Quaalude, she's gonna love me again." He could see no reason to even bother filming the rest of the scene as scripted. Pacino was incensed and, after a long argument, managed to convince De Palma that the soliloquy was crucial to both the scene and the film.

De Palma later acknowledged that Pacino's instincts had been right on the money. "Pacino has all sorts of ideas about how things should be done. So do I. We worked out that he was right about some things and so was I. Collectively we were always right." (Incidentally, De Palma did end up shortening the scene in the editing room, by cutting the whole build-up of Tony, Elvira and Manny sweeping into the restaurant; this included an amusing exchange where Tony spots a famous television anchorman at another table and gives him an inside scoop about 20 kilos of cocaine that has gone missing following a DEA drug bust.)

Aside from Stone, another member of the *Scarface* team expressed surprise at the leisurely pace of the shoot. Actor Gregg Henry had been cast in a tiny role as Charles Goodson, a shady Washington politician who is a guest at Sosa's mountain retreat in the scene where Tony Montana is instructed to help Alberto the Shadow (Mark Margolis) assassinate Orlando Gutierrez before he can deliver a speech at the United Nations. It was a very short, simple scene with no elaborate camera moves and Henry had only a single line of dialog: "How do you do, Mr Montana." As he observed: "I thought it would take two and half days to shoot that scene. It took more like two and a half weeks!"

What no one knew at the time was that the most grueling sequence of the entire *Scarface* shoot was yet to come—and it would throw the whole shooting schedule out of the window.

And it wasn't the infamous chainsaw murder sequence.

It was the climactic shootout with the Bolivian assassins at Tony Montana's mansion.

De Palma had allotted two weeks to shoot the climax to *Scarface*, feeling that he would need the time given the complex logistics of choreographing and filming the sequence.

The scene was to be shot on the sound stages at Universal, in the vast hallway which Scarfiotti had designed for the Coral Gables mansion, complete with a sweeping grand staircase and an indoor fountain, the centerpiece of which was an enormous golden globe in which the words 'The World is Yours' were spelled out in neon lettering. This catchphrase—the film's most explicit homage to the 1932 version of *Scarface*—had already appeared once in the movie, blinking on the side of an airship as part of an advertisement for Pan American airlines after Tony Montana has killed Frank Lopez and assumed his crown.

The sequence begins as Tony Montana returns home from the abortive assassination attempt of Gutierrez in New York. As he drives through the gates of Coral Gables, we can already see that Alejandro Sosa's Bolivian assassins have breached the security around the estate and are swarming through the grounds. Tony retires to his office on the first floor and has a final encounter with a deranged Gina. When one of the assassins shoots her, all hell breaks loose as Montana takes on the entire private army single-handedly. In the film's closing moments, he stands on the mezzanine of the mansion, shouting out his defiance, before being shot in the back and plummeting down into the fountain below.

De Palma and Alonzo utilized five cameras running simultaneously to catch all of the action: two at ground level with the Bolivians, one on the mezzanine with Pacino, a fourth on a crane to film events from above, and the fifth a special camera rigged to film in slow motion. As John Alonzo observed: "It probably took more than half a day to line up where the cameras were going to go."

Alonzo also took advantage of a new development from camera designers Panavision which was called Pancam. This allowed a regular 35mm film camera to be easily converted to shoot onto videotape. Thus De Palma would have the option, when he was editing the film, of either showing an event happening in color on film or in grainy monochrome like CCTV footage.

Special-effects technicians Stan Parks and Ken Pepiot dreamed up a clever gizmo in direct response to a request by De Palma for more photogenic firepower for the climax. De Palma wanted to know if it was possible to rig machine guns that would give more impressive muzzle flashes—the blinding flames expelled by the gun from its barrel as it fires —than were traditionally seen in movies. He felt the scene would have more impact if the muzzle flashes matched the actual speed and ferocity of the machine gun fire on the soundtrack.

In fact, the problem wasn't with the firearms. The problem was with the cameras. The muzzle flashes occurred at a faster rate than the speed of the camera shutter. Thus only a small percentage of the flashes were ever caught on film because most of them occurred when the shutter was closed. To resolve the problem, Parks and Pepiot devised a sequencing device that linked the machine guns to the cameras and only allowed the guns to fire when the shutter was open. Because the guns were now in perfect synchronization with the camera shutter, every muzzle flash would be caught on film.

However, there was one problem with Parks and Pepiot's ingenious device. Unless the guns were perfectly synchronized with the camera shutters, they wouldn't fire at all. The actors would pull the trigger, but nothing would happen. Al Pacino ended up losing his temper on several occasions because he wanted the freedom to be able to fire the gun when he felt like it, but was constantly having to stop in mid-performance until the guns were properly synchronized.

For Pacino, shooting the climax became an ordeal that never seemed any closer to reaching a conclusion. The sheer length of the shoot was already beginning to take its toll and Pacino was exhausted, yet had to maintain a stupefying level of energy for the finale as the berserk Montana single-handedly takes on the gang of assassins. As he described it: "The only memory I have of that is of putting myself in a kind of trance. I found myself every day going into this room with all the guns and all the smoke and all this hell. I would give myself a kind of mantra and I would go in, bite the bullet and spend 12 or 14 hours every day, day in and day out, shooting that sequence. If you can get into a rhythm and you are relaxed when you're doing it, you can do anything. You get Zen about it because if you for once look around you, it's just not endurable."

To further complicate matters, Pacino seriously burned his hand on the set one day when he mistakenly grabbed one of the prop guns by its barrel. Although the machine guns were rigged to shoot blanks, the barrels of the guns still became red hot when they were fired. Pacino was rushed to hospital with second-degree burns to the palm of his hand and De Palma was forced to spend two weeks shooting around the actor while he recovered.

The only moment of levity during the weeks it took to complete the sequence was when De Palma received an unexpected guest on the set. Steven Spielberg had let his old friend use his private offices at Universal for the duration of the *Scarface* shoot and decided to swing by and see how things were going. For a bit of fun, De Palma and Alonzo rigged up one of the cameras so that Spielberg could operate it. His sole contribution to the movie is a bug's eye view of the assassins as they race across the patio into the hallway of Montana's mansion.

As with everything connected with the film's climax, Tony Montana's death scene was anything but a simple matter to stage. Having been shot in the back on the mezzanine, Montana was to stagger to the edge of the balcony and plummet down into the fountain on the ground floor, allowing the camera to pull back to reveal his body floating in the water beneath the golden globe with its ironic message: "The World is Yours."

That stunt alone took two days to film. The stuntman not only had to take the fall face first into the fountain, but then had to remain immobile, holding his breath, while De Palma completed the slow, majestic crane shot that would signify the end of the film.

After all that, the thought of returning to Miami for a fortnight of location photography must have seemed like a holiday.

18

"Don't get high on your own supply."

Elvira Hancock

One of the most persistent myths that has grown up around the making of *Scarface* is that actual cocaine was being used on the set of the movie to enhance the performances.

These rumors were given added credence after Al Pacino, when directly asked about whether or not he was actually snorting coke during his sequences, chose to preserve his mystique by refusing to answer the question. He responded, "I don't like to give away that secret because it takes away from somebody's belief. You have to have a secret. That's part of what we do."

Brian De Palma, however, was less evasive on the subject, pointing out, "Had the coke been real, the whole budget of that movie would have been on his table at the end."

Pacino's coked-out frenzy at the end of the movie was simply good acting. "Pacino's very straight," De Palma said. "The idea that you have to be drunk to play drunk went out at the turn of the century."

Instead, lactose—powdered baby milk—was used as a substitute for the cocaine. In fact, lactose is frequently used by professional drug dealers to cut with cocaine in order to make it stretch farther. The lactose was perfectly safe for the cast to snort, although it tended to clog up the nostrils. "Al didn't like it," De Palma revealed. "It stuffed up his nose and he had to keep blowing it after scenes."

The other apocryphal tale usually connected with the production is that the infamous chainsaw sequence—in which Hector the Toad (Al Israel), the Colombian drug dealer, dismembers Tony Montana's friend Angel Fernandez (Pepe Serna) in a grubby hotel shower stall in the aftermath of a botched drug deal—had originally been filmed in all its gory detail but had been censored from the film.

From the outset, De Palma knew that the chainsaw scene, which occurs just 18 minutes into *Scarface*, was crucial to set the tone of the piece, in the same way that Angie Dickinson's explicit murder early on in *Dressed To Kill* had echoed through the rest of that movie. "Once you have set up a terrifically violent scene early in a movie, you don't have to do much more after that," he explained.

It was more a question of how much De Palma needed to show to get his point across. "I wanted to establish a level of violence that nobody had ever seen before. This was a whole different level of Mob interaction, not the pleasant shoot-outs, stranglings and people being stabbed through the hand of *The Godfather*. We were into *really* terrible ways of people killing each other. They didn't just kill each other in these drug wars, they literally chopped people up and they found them sawed up in a trashcan outside a 7-Eleven. We're in a whole different world here."

Behind-the-scenes photos taken during the filming of the scene do reveal that a fake severed arm was created for the movie—it can clearly be seen dangling from the shower rail—and Oliver Stone's script originally indicated that the sequence was to have continued with Hector sawing off Angel's leg. (There was also a brief scene in the script where Tony returns to the bathroom after shooting Hector and picks up the good luck charm that Angel was carrying. This was a reference to an earlier sequence where Tony berated Angel for being a superstitious fool while they were driving to Hector's motel. Neither scene made it into the finished film.)

However, De Palma decided early on that the sequence was predominantly going to happen offscreen. "When you do a scene like that there are props around that you use or don't use," he explains. "Though we may have had body parts around, we either shot them and never used them, or simply didn't use them. The intention was always to suggest what was happening. You could hear it; you didn't have to see it. I just had to figure out a way of doing it that wouldn't turn into *The Texas Chain Saw Massacre.*" (This final comment would seem to suggest that De Palma had not actually seen *The Texas Chain Saw Massacre* (1974), as that film's director, Tobe Hooper, did not show any of the chainsaw attacks onscreen either. Working on the tightest of budgets, Hooper simply couldn't afford any elaborate make-up or special effects. Like De Palma, he had allowed the viewer's imagination to do all the work through judicious editing and the use of sound effects.)

In a very early cut of the film, De Palma did leave in around twelve frames showing Angel's arm being sawn off. However, even that brief glimpse had been removed by the time the film was screened for the censors. All that was present in the final cut of the movie was the image of blood spraying on Angel's face, before De Palma cut to a reaction shot of Pacino. Afterwards, all the audience can see are the blood-splattered tiles of the bathroom walls.

The scene was considerably less grueling to film than it is to watch, thanks to the director's instinctive knowledge of precisely how much he would have to show to get the desired effect. As Al Pacino noted: "That is a vintage De Palma technique and you can feel it when you're doing it. He sets things up in such a way, with such a strong visual understanding of how he wanted to build it. It was so completely mapped out that it wasn't difficult to do."

The exteriors to the chainsaw scene were amongst the few sequences that were actually shot on location in Miami when the *Scarface* crew returned there for two weeks at the very end of the shooting schedule. The location selected for the scene was the Sun Ray Apartments at 728 Ocean Drive in Miami Beach. (The building, incidentally, is still standing, although virtually unrecognizable today. A few years after the film was made, the property was given a facelift and converted into Johnny Rocket's Restaurant.)

When the crew returned to Miami, Martin Bregman was sufficiently concerned about the possibility of reprisals from the Cuban community that he hired heavy security to monitor the cast and crew while they were on location.

It all proved to be unnecessary, as the final few days of filming passed without incident.

19

"I never fucked anybody over in my life
didn't have it coming to them."

Tony Montana

When production concluded on *Scarface* in the spring of
1983, Brian De Palma immediately began whittling down the
miles of footage that had been shot, trying to get a handle on
the shape of the final film.

Scarface was scheduled for a Christmas release in the
United States. This was the prime period for new movies
hoping to nab Oscar nominations for the following year. By
opening at this time, the film would be still be fresh in voters'
minds, and in the case of the film actually grabbing some
nominations or, even better, winning some awards, the
accolades would give it an extra boost at the box office.
Following its roadshow presentation in the US, *Scarface* was
then slated to roll out into foreign territories early the
following year.

This schedule gave De Palma a generous six months in
which to cut and score the film prior to release.

Editing the film was Gerald B Greenberg, who had
previously worked with De Palma on *Dressed To Kill* and would
go on to cut many of the director's subsequent films. De Palma
trusted Greenberg implicitly. "I can just talk to him on the phone
and he'll know exactly what I want. And can even do it better."

More of an unknown quantity was the composer who had been selected to score the *Scarface* soundtrack. Although De Palma generally favored orchestral scores and tended to select classical composers for his films—Bernard Herrmann for *Sisters* and *Obsession*, John Williams for *The Fury*, Pino Donaggio for *Carrie, Dressed To Kill,* and *Blow Out*—he had agreed to get Italian pop producer-turned-composer Giorgio Moroder to provide the music for *Scarface*.

Although he was primarily known for being one of the architects of the 1970s disco sound, Moroder had recently become Hollywood's composer du jour. Much of this had to do with the ways that films were marketed in the late 1970s and 1980s. Prior to that, original soundtrack albums were seen as a specialist area of the music business, of appeal only to ardent cinephiles. Aside from musicals and a few noteworthy exceptions such as the rock soundtrack to *Easy Rider* (1969) or the soul soundtracks for *Shaft* (1970) and *Superfly* (1971), soundtrack albums were seldom taken that seriously.

But when the soundtracks to films such as *Saturday Night Fever* (1977), *Thank God It's Friday* (1978), and *Grease* (1978) began to top the album charts, Hollywood began to appreciate their value. A bestselling soundtrack album not only brought in extra revenue for the film, but a hit song lifted from the soundtrack also served as free advertising for a movie in the all-important youth market.

Giorgio Moroder was seen as having the Midas touch with movie soundtracks. Not only had his anthemic score for *Midnight Express* won him an Oscar for Best Score, but he had enjoyed hit singles from a number of his films, including "Call Me" by Blondie from the soundtrack of *American Gigolo*,

"Cat People (Putting Out Fire)" by David Bowie from Paul Schrader's *Cat People* update, and "Flashdance… What a Feeling" by Irene Cara from *Flashdance*. It was a seemingly unbeatable combination.

De Palma had heard and liked Moroder's score for *American Gigolo* and thought his sound was ideal for *Scarface*. In the same way that he had steered John Alonzo and Ferdinando Scarfiotti out of the darkness towards bright lighting and primary colors, he wanted Moroder's music to capture the Miami of the 1980s. "In the clubs, all they played was this endless coked-up disco music, so that seemed perfect," he explained. "I thought it should have that very electric, disco sound. That's what they were playing in the clubs. That's what these people lived by. It's a very 'cocaine' sound. You get in one of these places, put down a couple of lines, turn the music up until everybody can hardly breathe, and party!"

Moroder fulfilled his brief a little too well. If Universal executives had been hoping for a hit single from the *Scarface* soundtrack they were to be sorely disappointed. Most of the songs in the film—such as the Babylon Club dancefloor numbers "She's On Fire" and "Dance Dance Dance", not to mention the frivolous "Shake It Up", which plays during the chainsaw sequence—were mindless bubblegum pop that was an ordeal to listen to once, let alone repeatedly on the radio. The only other notable song in the film, "Scarface (Push It To The Limit)", which played over a montage of scenes marking Tony Montana's rise to infamy, including his marriage to Elvira, the spreading tentacles of his business empire, and the opening of his sister Gina's beauty salon—was a cheesy and eminently forgettable soft rock number performed by Paul Engemann that still seems entirely out of place in the movie. (The song was later released as a 12″ promo disc by MCA Records and is now considered something of a collectors' item.)

Moroder's incidental music is far more memorable and evocative. His theme for Tony Montana is a slow, brooding electronic pulse that helps propel the sequences in which it appears into new levels of danger. Moroder said, "The theme for Tony had to reflect the character and personality of Al Pacino in the movie. It had to be dangerous, a little suspenseful, but a little deep too." His themes for Elvira and Gina were effectively variations on a theme that subtly suggested Tony's incestuous longings. "The theme for the two girls was a little tricky because I wanted to have the same feel for both, because Tony was in love with his sister and in love with Elvira. So the sounds are very similar but the melodies are slightly different, to create a little ambiguity."

One other footnote in the *Scarface* saga was the issuing of a paperback movie tie-in by the Berkley Publishing Group in 1983. As with soundtrack albums, the official movie tie-in had become an essential element of a film's marketing strategy, free advertising dropped into every book store around the world. In the case of a title based on a bestselling novel, such as *The Godfather* or *Carrie*, it was simply a case of re-issuing the existing novel with a new cover featuring the poster artwork from the movie, with perhaps a small pictorial insert showing a selection of production stills.

For *Scarface*, however, it wasn't really possible to repackage and reissue Armitage Trail's 1930 novel given that it bore so little resemblance to the new film. More to the point, movie tie-ins were often issued to fit in with publisher's schedules rather than a film's release date. Quite often the book would go on sale weeks before the movie opened in theaters and many people couldn't resist reading the story before they saw the film. If someone were to read Trail's clunky and old fashioned book before they saw the glossy update, it might actually put them off the film entirely.

Instead, the writer Paul Monette was commissioned to write an original novel based entirely upon Oliver Stone's screenplay. Monette was a poet and novelist who had turned to writing screenplays and movie tie-ins as a lucrative sideline to his verse and fiction. None of his screenplays were ever brought to the screen, but his novelizations for films such *Nosferatu the Vampyre* (1979), *Predator* (1987) and *Midnight Run* (1988) were very successful. Although Monette would later become one of the most powerful and influential writers on the subject of AIDS (he would himself succumb to AIDS-related complications in 1995), at the time of *Scarface* he was just another writer pursuing his muse.

One of the most curious aspects of the movie tie-in is that they are frequently written while a project is still in production and before the writer has had a chance to see the finished film (there have even been cases where the novel and film end differently purely because the film's ending was changed after the book went to print). Part of the art of writing such a book is to be able to take a screenplay and imagine every aspect of the performances, direction and cinematography without the benefit of having experienced them first-hand. For *Scarface*, Monette's book includes several scenes that were present in Oliver Stone's screenplay but never made it to the final cut of the movie. It also, by necessity, includes a few scenes that have come straight from Monette's imagination, to either bridge gaps in the narrative or explain elements of the plot that were only implied by Stone and De Palma.

A second edition of Monette's *Scarface* novelization was published in December of 1983 by Sphere Books in the UK.

The editing process proceeded smoothly, without any major upsets.

De Palma was forced to sacrifice a handful of scenes in order to keep *Scarface* down to a manageable running time. Most of these were sequences from the Freedomtown camp at the very start of the film, which were deemed to be superfluous and slowed down the progress of the story. Aside from cutting the references to Tony and Manny watching and discussing *The Treasure of the Sierra Madre*, De Palma also removed a lengthy scene in which Tony attempts to contact his mother from the telephone callboxes in the camp and another scene where he rebuffs the advances of one of the gay internees.

Two other scenes, which occurred much later in the film, were also removed entirely because they added little to the story. One revolved around Tony and Manny hiring the services of a shifty lawyer with a fistful of cash; the other was an amusing scene that preceded the assassination attempt on Gutierrez in New York and showed Tony distracting some nosy cops by pretending to be searching for his missing dog. And in the same way that De Palma shortened the "Say good night to the bad guy" restaurant sequence by removing the earlier encounter with the television anchorman, he also reduced the length of Tony's first visit to see his mother and Gina at their house.

While none of these scenes appeared in the movie when it was first screened in theaters, a few were later reinstated for the abridged version which aired on airlines and on network television, to make up for footage that had had to be edited for violence.

De Palma's final cut of the movie clocked in at just under 170 minutes.

When *Scarface* was finally completed, De Palma had very little to do with the film's marketing or promotion, beyond pointing out a mistake in the poster artwork.

The Universal advertising department had devised a stark black-and-white poster for the movie, bearing the slogan: "He loved the American Dream. With a Vengeance".

"When they have Al Pacino as a gangster, to the advertising department it's another *Godfather* because of the success of those films," De Palma said. "But I remember specifically looking at the ad campaign and they had Al in a black suit, holding a gun. And I said 'This is not a black suit Mafia guy, this is a white suit Cuban gangster.' So they reversed the suit so that it was a white suit, and that was the little effect I had on the merchandising or the selling of the movie."

It's a tribute to the iconic nature of the poster and the resilience of its imagery that it remains in print today and can be bought at numerous movie memorabilia stores (an actual original American one-sheet or British quad poster dating from 1983 will cause a sizeable dent in your wallet in the collector's market). The poster image was slightly amended for the film's subsequent release on home video, which added the figure of Michelle Pfeiffer into the background, to capitalise on the fact that she had been catapulted to stardom by the movie.

In recent years, a small cottage industry has developed that specializes in posters from *Scarface*, usually depicting Tony Montana in classic poses from the movie—slumped in his desk at Coral Gables behind a mountain of cocaine, gazing out at the Pan-American blimp from the window of Frank Lopez's mansion, or wielding his "little friend" the grenade launcher. When Al Pacino visited London in 2004 for the premiere of *The Merchant of Venice*, he was bemused when various people in the crowd outside the theater presented him with copies of such posters to be autographed.

More than Michael Corleone in *The Godfather* saga, Tony Montana in *Scarface* is fast becoming Pacino's defining performance.

Having finished work on his director's cut of the movie, Brian De Palma and Martin Bregman screened the film for the cast and crew. Despite all the pain that had gone into the film's making, Al Pacino was impressed with the final result. "When I first saw the movie I thought Brian had achieved that operatic style. I thought it would be controversial. I thought that there would be reaction to it, that it would effect a certain kind of criticism. But it was the movie Brian set out to make and I thought he achieved it. I was pleased."

One person, however, was not entirely convinced by the movie.

Oliver Stone, who had been on hand to observe the film at every stage of its inception, was sorely disappointed. He had written the film as a critique of capitalism and the American Dream, but felt that this message had been lost along the way. "The politics in it are buried by a lot of superficial trivia," he observed. "To some it's a movie about cars, palaces, money and coke. It's not just about that. It's about what those things do to you and how they corrupt you. That theme got lost."

He also noted: "I don't think Brian De Palma was as interested as I was in exploring the Hispanic community. I spent a lot of time in Miami, I got interested in Spanish culture, which helped me later with *Salvador*. I always had the impression that what Brian wanted was to make a genre film. It didn't much matter to him whether the gangsters were Italian, Greek, Irish or Cuban."

Having been cut out of the loop by John Milius during the making of *Conan the Barbarian*, Stone took advantage of his intimate knowledge of the *Scarface* shoot to write a fifteen-page critique of De Palma's cut, making suggestions about how he felt the film had failed to live up to its potential and how it could be improved. He gave copies of this missive to De Palma and Bregman, who agreed to take his notes on board.

Unfortunately, he also sent a copy to Al Pacino.

When Bregman and De Palma discovered what Stone had done, they were furious. Having the screenwriter present during filming had seemed like a good idea at the time, but now their decision had come back to bite them.

Both of them were aware that *Scarface* was a hugely controversial project and stood a good chance of alienating viewers as a result of its uncompromising nature. The last thing they needed was someone sowing seeds of doubt in the mind of the film's lead actor as to the film's perceived failings, be they artistic or commercial. They felt that Stone had overstepped the mark.

Stone remained defiant. "Marty and Brian got really upset because I told Al this stuff. They were afraid that he would go crazy on them. But you have to deal with actors on the cut. You can't run away from them. They figured the less said, the better."

Stone's incautious remarks caused a serious rift between the writer and his fellow film-makers which soured their relations for a long time afterwards.

In the meantime, Bregman and De Palma had a more pressing problem to occupy them.

How to get *Scarface* past the censors.

part three:

the final cut

20

"You think you can take me?
You need a fuckin' army if you gonna take me."

Tony Montana

Howard Hawks's version of *Scarface* had been held up for more than a year because of censorship problems with Will Hays and the MPPDA.

Over half a century later, the MPPDA had been replaced by Motion Picture Association of America (MPAA) and its Classification and Ratings Administration (CARA). Standards had eased to the extent that the MPAA were no longer in a position to veto a screenplay before it was filmed, nor were they in a position to refuse to allow a film to be released. All they could do was give it a rating as to its suitability for a particular audience. In the 1980s, CARA could give a film one of four ratings: a G was awarded to films suitable for all audiences; PG stood for Parental Guidance and indicated that the film might contain material unsuitable for young children; R meant Restricted and that anyone under the age of 17 was required to be accompanied by an adult; and X meant adults only.

Yet if the ratings system had changed, so had the marketplace. With the rise of hardcore pornography in America in the 1970s, the X rating became synonymous with porn and now came with a stigma attached. Many chains refused to book X-rated movies regardless of whether or not they were pornographic. Similarly, many periodicals and TV stations refused to run ads for X-rated films. If a film could only be shown in a limited number of theaters and couldn't be advertised, it had a detrimental effect on its box-office potential. Just a few years earlier, movies such as *Midnight Cowboy* (1969), *A Clockwork Orange* (1971), *Last Tango in Paris* (1972), and even Brian De Palma's *Greetings* had all been rated X and it had not affected their popularity one iota. *Midnight Cowboy* had even won the Oscar for Best Film. But times had changed and most directors were contractually obliged to present a film that would be, at the very most, rated R. And they were expected to cut anything out of the film that stood in its way of getting that R rating.

Whilst it is not and has never been mandatory to get MPAA approval for a film, the only alternative at the time of *Scarface* would have been to release it unrated. This had worked for George A Romero's low-budget horror satire *Dawn of the Dead*, which Romero chose to release unrated in 1979 when he could not secure an R rating from the MPAA without cutting his film. In *Dawn of the Dead*'s case, the unrated status gave the movie a certain cachet among horror fans and confirmed Romero's status as a maverick film-maker. In 1990, CARA introduced the NC-17 rating—which indicated that no one under the age of 17 could be admitted—for films of an adult, but not pornographic, nature. However, even now, the NC-17 rating stigmatizes a film and makes it difficult to release and promote except in very specialized markets.

Brian De Palma and Martin Bregman knew they were going to have a fight on their hands with *Scarface*. It wasn't just the level of violence in the film, but also the language. With the word "fuck" being uttered more than 200 times during the course of the movie, it not only established, as De Palma put it, "a level of violence that nobody had ever seen before", it also established a level of profanity that nobody had ever heard before.

De Palma also felt that the CARA chairman Richard Heffner would be gunning for him. The pair had locked horns just a few years previously over *Dressed To Kill*, which had originally been rated X and which De Palma had been forced to cut heavily to secure an R. De Palma had not accepted CARA's decision graciously and had gone on record many times since to decry the entire ratings system.

What angered De Palma was the arbitrariness of the MPAA's ratings policy. Because they did not consider themselves to be censors but were merely classifying the films, they were not obliged to point out specific problem areas. As De Palma saw it, a film-maker was meant to blindly make adjustments to the film in line with vague comments about "cumulative violence" or "explicit sexuality". no one would tell you exactly what you had to cut to secure an R rating, simply that you had to cut something. Many film-makers had taken to purposely shooting more violence and flesh than was necessary, just so that they would have something to cut out later to appease CARA.

Neither Bregman nor De Palma were entirely surprised when their preferred cut of *Scarface* was presented to CARA for classification and was returned with an X. De Palma duly made a few edits to the movie to reduce the violence and resubmitted it to CARA. They returned it with another X. De

Palma made some more edits. CARA watched the film again and returned it with yet another X. De Palma made even more edits. The film was still rated X.

The situation had become farcical.

"The studio were saying to me 'Solve this'," De Palma explained but, with the film's December release date drawing ever closer, he was seemingly unable to do anything to appease CARA. Even when he convinced CARA to detail the areas which concerned them, he found himself going in circles. "We would fix one part and then they would suddenly raise questions about another part that they'd never mentioned before."

At one point, CARA began questioning the scene that depicted the shootout in the Babylon Club. When the gunfight breaks out, a comedy mime artist is performing in the club and is shown getting caught in the crossfire. "They were fixated on how many gun hits were in the clown," De Palma laughs. "I remember thinking 'The clown? You're worried about the number of gun hits in *the clown?*'"

De Palma felt the cuts he was being forced to make were seriously affecting the intent of his film. "The movie was *supposed* to be shocking. It's a shocking world. These are like gangsters you've never seen before."

Martin Bregman supported De Palma and pointed out that the violence and language were far from gratuitous. "You go to a playground in New York City and listen to the nine-year-olds. You'll hear some words. A kid going to this movie isn't going to go out and contact his local cocaine dealer. We painted that world as bad as it is."

Even the president of the MPAA, Jack Valenti, went on record praising the film's anti-drug message.

De Palma had had enough. "After the fourth submission, I said to Universal, 'This is crazy. It's hurting the movie aesthetically and commercially. I'm not doing any more cutting.' I got on the phone and I called some of my reporter friends that nobody knew about and I said 'This is an outrage'."

The result were scores of articles in which De Palma vented his anger at CARA and the MPAA, explicitly stating that Richard Heffner was just using *Scarface* as a way of exacting a personal vendetta against the director. Heffner gave the accusations short shrift. "I appreciate the publicity value of attacks on the mean old censor, but we rate films not filmmakers. On the invisible scale which we carry in our heads, we felt *Scarface* deserved something stronger than an R. The accumulation of violence and language was just too much. We consider ourselves responsible to parents and we didn't think many parents would cheer us for giving this film an R."

Having reached an apparent impasse, Bregman decided that the only way to resolve the situation would be through arbitration, to present the film to the MPAA's appeals board and request that they reverse the decision by CARA. The appeals board consisted of Jack Valenti and a committee of studio executives, film distributors and theater owners. It was a tricky situation because, if Bregman and De Palma lost the appeal, Universal would have the right to take the film out of their hands and simply cut it as they saw fit.

De Palma was bullish about the situation and argued that, if the appeal failed, he would take the case to the US Supreme Court. "I spoke to a lawyer who suggested that if I were to bring a lawsuit against the rating system, I might win. It's restraint of trade."

Bregman, however, was determined to leave nothing to chance. "I went prepared for, literally, a court case."

The appeals hearing was set for November 8.

As witnesses, Bregman recruited experts from various fields. Jay Cocks, the film critic for *Time* magazine, defended the film on aesthetic grounds. Major Nick Novarro of the Florida police force validated every act of violence depicted in the film as being an accurate representation of crime in Miami and its environs. Two child psychiatrists, Dr H Feinberg and Dr Richard Atkins, testified that the film was suitable for viewing by any child over the age of thirteen. Bob Rehme, the head of distribution at Universal Pictures, also attended in support of the film.

The appeals board overturned the X rating.

"We conducted this like a trial and we beat them," Bregman said. "We beat them hands down. The vote was eighteen to two in favor of our getting an R rating."

De Palma has acknowledged that this very public battle with the censors has resulted in one major misconception about *Scarface*. "Because I cut back the picture three times, everybody assumes they saw the final cut. But I called the head of the studio and I said 'If I have an X on the first version and I still have an X in the last version, why don't I just go with the first version?' They said 'No, no, no. You can't do that.' I said 'Why not? An X is an X, isn't it?' So the version you see of *Scarface* is the original version I cut. It has not been changed. It has not been cut back. That's what we fought over and that's what we won with."

The British censors, however, proved less amenable. When the British Board of Film Classification viewed *Scarface* in late 1983, the late James Ferman, then the President of the organization, requested eleven seconds of cuts to the chainsaw scene.

Although the BBFC were prepared to allow through the sequence in which Angel's arm was severed, they requested that Hector the Toad's subsequent sneering aside "Now the leg, eh?" and the following shot of Pacino and the shower curtain being sprayed with blood be removed in their entirety.

In the end, Brian De Palma himself approved a slightly longer edit. Along with the eleven seconds that the BBFC had requested be removed, he also opted to cut the preceding thirteen seconds—which entailed a cutaway shot of Manny sitting in the car outside the Sun Ray Apartments and getting the brush-off from a blonde in a turquoise bikini. Thus the British prints of *Scarface* that went into release in the spring of 1984, issued with an 18 Certificate by the BBFC, lost 24 seconds of footage in total.

It isn't hard to see why De Palma ended up cutting more rather than less. Had he stuck with the BBFC's recommendations, it would have resulted in an awkward jump cut in the middle of the scene. By volunteering to remove the further thirteen seconds, there is a much more fluid transition from Pacino's reaction to Angel's arm being severed to Manny and Chi Chi (Angel Salazar) intuiting that something has gone wrong with the drug deal, jumping out of the car and crossing the road to the motel.

Although the removal of what, to all intents and purposes, is a fairly inexplicit moment might be seen as simple nitpicking by the BBFC, it should be remembered that in the mid-1980s the UK was going though one of its periodic censorious phases. The overly liberal attitude adopted by the British censors during the late 1970s had led to a general tightening of standards in the following decade. There had already been numerous reports in the press about De Palma's travails with the America censors over *Scarface* and, in the absence of anything better to do, the British conservative tabloid newspapers started bleating about the allegedly excessive levels of violence in the film and demanding that it be banned. This was despite the fact, of course, that no one in the UK had even seen the finished film at that point.

Ever aware of adverse publicity, the BBFC's James Ferman would occasionally make a token cut to a controversial film for no other reason than to pre-empt any future criticism. Were the controversy to arise again at a later date, Ferman could defuse the situation by pointing out that the supposedly worst excesses in the film had already been removed, even if, as in the case of *Scarface*, those changes were purely superficial. Very few tabloid journalists could be bothered to look in microscopic detail at precisely what cuts had been made, nor to analyze how they affected the film as a whole.

For anyone intimately familiar with *Scarface*, it's interesting to do a side-by-side comparison of the cut and uncut versions of the chainsaw scene. In one respect, the scene was slightly improved and even intensified by the edit, as the shot of Pacino being soaked with blood as Angel's leg is being severed offscreen was never entirely convincing, looking for all the world as if the actor was simply being sprayed by a squirt gun just out of the range of the camera.

Whatever the case, all of the censored footage was quietly restored to *Scarface* for its re-issue on video in 1994 with the approval of the BBFC, and all copies of the film now in circulation in the UK are identical to Brian De Palma's final cut.

And in what can be seen as a sign of the ever-evolving standards of the viewing public, the fully uncut *Scarface* has even been screened on prime time British network television without arousing any significant resistance or eliciting more than a handful of complaints.

21

"Can't you stop saying 'fuck' all the time?"

Elvira Hancock

Of all the comments made about *Scarface* before and after its release, the most perceptive came from Martin Scorsese, who sat in for a special screening arranged by Bregman and De Palma for the cast, crew and friends. Halfway through the film, Scorsese leaned back to Steven Bauer, who was seated behind him, and whispered, "You know, they're gonna hate this film. But they're gonna love it too."

With very few exceptions, the critics hated it.

Rex Reed in the *New York Post* wrote: "The violence is endless, the four-letter words take the place of the English language, the actors work vigorously, the decadence and perversion drown everything in a vicious grunge. When it's over, you feel mugged, debased, like you've eaten a bad clam." Even Pauline Kael, a longtime De Palma supporter, reported in *The New Yorker*: "*Scarface* has the length of an epic but not the texture of an epic and its dramatic arc is faulty… This may be the only action picture that turns into an allegory of impotence." The foreign critics were no less dismissive. In London, *The Daily Telegraph* newspaper said of De Palma, "The attempt at the big picture seems to find him far out of his depth."

However, the movie did find a handful of supporters. *Variety* described it as "a grandiose morality play, excessive, broad and operatic at times." David Ansen in *Newsweek* reported: "What makes *Scarface* so satisfying is the obvious relish with which De Palma tells his first epic-size tale... It's a grand, shallow, decadent entertainment, which like all good Hollywood gangster movies delivers the punch and counterpunch of glamor and disgust." And Vincent Canby in the *New York Times* described it as "A relentlessly bitter, satirical tale of greed, in which all supposedly decent emotions are sent up for the possible ways in which they can be perverted."

When the film opened on December 9, 1983, audiences were similarly divided.

Hardcore De Palma fans were disappointed by a film that featured none of the director's trademarks: the intricate plotting, the stylish camerawork, or the elaborate set pieces. *Scarface* not only seemed loud, vulgar and overlit, but also just plain anonymous.

Mainstream audiences felt that Al Pacino had demeaned himself with the film, wasting his talents on a crass, sensationalist potboiler. They were appalled by the relentless carnage, the barrage of profane language and the general tone of amorality.

Just about everyone complained that the film was overlong and that it dragged painfully during Tony Montana's long downward spiral into coked-out oblivion.

One specific source of scorn was the end credit: "This film is dedicated to Howard Hawks and Ben Hecht." Many film critics and cineastes were outraged at the chutzpah displayed by Brian De Palma in even mentioning his overblown exploitation flick in the same breath as Hecht and Hawks's masterpiece. But they seemed to have forgotten that the 1932 version of *Scarface* had been vilified for its violence every bit as much as the 1983 version.

De Palma already had an inkling from its preview screenings that audiences were not going to take to the film. At one such screening, he even refused to look at the audience response cards afterwards. "Believe me, you didn't want to be around for the preview of *Scarface*," he later laughed. "Or the opening. People were outraged—you saw people running up the aisle. I remember the opening night party; I thought they were going to skin me alive."

One of the few people who escaped the critical mauling was Michelle Pfeiffer, who won unanimous praise despite the thankless nature of her role. She responded by defending the film vociferously: "I know it's not an easy film to watch, but since it's an anti-drug film I think it had to get violent to get the message across. Four-letter words? I'm so used to hearing that word that it doesn't really offend me. I use it myself, after all. And after fifteen minutes I don't think you are aware of it any more in the movie."

In a repeat of the furore that had accompanied the release of *Dressed To Kill*, De Palma was called upon to defend the film's violence. His response was as blunt as always: "We live in a society of free will. You don't have to look at it. Nobody had to go and see *Scarface*. Nobody held a gun to anybody's head. I have no sympathy for people who are shocked and ask how that kind of thing can exist. Hey, just read the ads. Caution: excessive language and maybe excessive violence. Be warned. I have a reputation for certain kinds of movies."

De Palma was bemused by suggestions that scenes such as the chainsaw murder were somehow excessive: "I think we underplayed the violence. The drug world is much more violent, brutal and cruel. We made no attempt to romanticize it, which is why we got so many negative opinions."

What everyone but a handful of critics seemed to miss—or perhaps chose to ignore—was the film's sense of irony. As fellow director Quentin Tarantino was to point out many years later, Brian De Palma is actually one of the "greatest satirists" in Hollywood. Both Oliver Stone and De Palma himself maintained that *Scarface* was a left-wing film, ruthlessly attacking what they perceived as the self-destructive nature of capitalism and the culture of excess in Reagan-era America.

De Palma was frustrated because he felt that the film was misunderstood: "Everyone focused on the violence of *Scarface* and missed the point—which was the American Dream gone awry. Violence is endemic to anyone who cuts corners and rides fast in the cocaine world. How is this multi-billion dollar industry allowed to go on in our society? But then you're addressing the tenets of capitalism, and who wants to be a pinko and come down on capitalist enterprise? Profit is its own justification in our society."

He also took the critics to task for suggesting that the use of mountains of cocaine was obviously exaggerated. "I've read those reviews and I don't think those people know anything about cocaine," he said. "A lot people I know in Hollywood are ex-cocaine addicts. They've come up to me and told me 'Yeah, it's exactly like that.' They've got the piles of cocaine on the table at parties that are every bit as big as the one Pacino had.

"The 1970s was the era of cocaine. It was an insider's drug. Nobody was into dreaming any more. They were moving faster, making more phone calls.

"It's the perfect capitalist drug."

22

"Every day above ground is a good day."

Mel Bernstein

There is a perception that *Scarface* was a box-office flop at the time of its theatrical release.

If you look at the US box office figures for the films released in 1983, *Scarface* sits at number 16 with a domestic box office gross of $44,668,798, trailing just behind *Jaws 3* ($45 million), *Superman III* ($59 million), and *Mr Mom* ($64 million), but a very long way behind the year's top grossers, *Terms of Endearment* ($108 million) and *Return of the Jedi* ($252 million). It must have been a source of chagrin to Brian De Palma that *Flashdance*, the film from which he had resigned, took the number three position with a take of $92,921,203.

On its opening weekend in the US, *Scarface* took $4,597,536 from 996 screens. It opened in second place to *Sudden Impact*, the film that marked Clint Eastwood's return to the role of maverick cop 'Dirty' Harry Callahan after a break of seven years. *Sudden Impact* took double the figure of *Scarface*, but had the advantage of opening at more than 1,500 screens. It should also be noted that the 170-minute running time of *Scarface* also had an effect on its earning potential as theaters would have had to reduce the number of daily screenings.

Both *Sudden Impact* and *Scarface* maintained the same chart positions the following week, although business for both dropped off by approximately 25 percent. By the Christmas weekend, *Scarface* had dropped to third place, but business had improved by 1.6 percent. *Scarface* was to remain in the box-office top ten until the end of January 1984.

But these numbers only tell part of the story.

In Hollywood accounting, a film is only considered to have recouped its costs when it has made back double its budget in box-office returns. *Scarface*, which had cost $25 million, was thus running at a loss according to its domestic box-office results. However, this does not take into account the film's international box office, which can often triple or even quadruple a film's overall tally. *Scarface* was a film that played in most foreign territories. Although the exact box-office figures for these markets are unavailable, it seems more than likely the film would have turned a substantial profit.

Al Pacino believes the misconception that *Scarface* was a flop came as a direct result of the controversy that had dogged the production from the outset: the news stories about the battles with the Cuban community in Miami, the outraged reports about the film's violence and the almost overwhelmingly negative response it received from the critics.

"*Scarface* was a huge success," he avows. "It's interesting how films are perceived. You can be in a movie and the perception is that it's a successful movie even if it isn't making any money. But there's a certain amount of copy on it and it is perceived as a success. With *Scarface*, it was such a controversial venture that it wasn't perceived as a successful movie, but it's actually one of the most successful movies I've ever made."

The film was snubbed by the Academy of Motion Picture Arts and Sciences and received no Oscar nominations. It did, however, receive three nominations at the Golden Globes, for Al Pacino, Steven Bauer and Giorgio Moroder.

Brian De Palma also received a nomination as Worst Director at the annual Razzie Awards celebrating Hollywood's worst movies.

He lost out to John Derek for *Bolero*.

Whether or not one considers *Scarface* to have been a failure, whether it be artistically or commercially, its notoriety had no lasting effect on any members of the cast or crew.

Immediately after *Scarface* was released, Columbia Pictures snapped up Brian De Palma for a three-picture deal that included his own office and parking space on the studio lot. De Palma was already talking up a storm over his next project, an erotic thriller set in the world of hardcore pornography entitled *Body Double*. Inspired by an incident on the set of *Dressed To Kill*, where De Palma had used the body of *Penthouse* Pet of the Year Victoria Lynn Johnson to double for Angie Dickinson during her shower rape scene, the film revolved around an out-of-work actor (Craig Wasson) hired to house-sit in a luxurious Los Angeles bachelor pad and who inadvertently witnesses the murder of one of the neighbors (Deborah Shelton). Following his tiny role in *Scarface*, Gregg Henry was given the meaty role of the killer this time round. Melanie Griffith, then the wife of Steven Bauer, played a porn star up to her neck in what turns out to be a murderous conspiracy.

Body Double was yet another of De Palma's spins on Alfred Hitchcock's *Rear Window* and *Vertigo* (with a playfully gory shower scene thrown in for good measure), only with considerably more sex and violence (the murder weapon selected by the killer is a huge phallic power drill). Although De Palma had earlier goaded the censors with the promise: "If they want an X, they'll get a *real* X," the film did manage, in the end, to get an R rating (in the UK, it only received an X rating after heavy cuts by the BBFC). However, it couldn't find an audience and proved to be an even bigger flop than *Blow Out*. Immediately afterwards, Columbia tore up De Palma's contract and closed his office at the studio.

Since then, De Palma has spent two decades bouncing between lavish, but decidedly anonymous, studio blockbusters such as *The Untouchables* (1987), *The Bonfire of the Vanities* (1990), and *Mission To Mars* (2000), and smaller, more typical thrillers such as *Raising Cain* (1992), *Snake Eyes* (1998), and *Femme Fatale* (2002). His biggest hit to date has been the big screen update of the 1960s TV series *Mission: Impossible* (1996), starring Tom Cruise.

By the time *Scarface* was released, Oliver Stone was already working on two more screenplays. *8 Million Ways To Die* was eventually brought to the screen by director Hal Ashby in 1986 and virtually disowned by its writer. *Year of the Dragon* (1985) was an altogether more pleasant experience working in collaboration with director Michael Cimino, although Stone maintained that producer Dino de Laurentiis eviscerated his preferred version of the script and the finished film once again brought with it charges of racism, this time from the Chinese community in America.

Stone silenced his critics by writing and directing *Salvador* (1986), a staunchly left wing critique of American intervention in Latin America that finally put him on the map as a serious film-maker. That same year also saw the release of

Platoon, which assured him a place on the A-list in Hollywood by winning the Oscars for Best Director and Best Film the following year. Films such as *Talk Radio* (1988), *Born on the Fourth of July* (1989), *JFK* (1991), *Natural Born Killers* (1994), and *Nixon* (1995) have ensured that Stone remains one of the most outspoken, overtly political and unapologetically controversial of modern American film-makers

Martin Bregman followed up *Scarface* with the genial comedy *Sweet Liberty* (1986), written, directed by and starring another of his former clients from his days as a personal manager, Alan Alda. He also used the movie to provide Michelle Pfeiffer with another nudge up the ladder to stardom by giving her the chance to prove her abilities as a light comedy actress in this tale of a film production company trying to shoot a movie about the American War of Independence in a sleepy backwoods town. Since then he has enjoyed his fair share of hits—*Sea of Love* (1989), *Matilda* (1996), and *The Bone Collector* (1999)—and misses—*Blue Ice* (1992), *The Shadow* (1994), and *Pluto Nash* (2002).

For Al Pacino, *Scarface* was the movie which opened him up as an actor. Up until that point, he had always fallen back on introspection in his cinema roles, a thoughtful rather than physical actor. After *Scarface*, he wasn't afraid to go for broke and chew up the scenery if the need arose. Although this has undoubtedly led to some of his most outrageously hammy turns—it's hard not to think of him in movies such as *Devil's Advocate* (1997), *The Recruit* (2003), and *Gigli* (2003) without wincing—any director who is prepared to keep him on a tight leash can bring out a genuinely galvanizing performance, such as in *Glengarry Glen Ross* (1992), *Heat*

(1995), and *The Insider* (1999). Ironically, Pacino finally won his Oscar for Best Actor in one of his lesser roles, as the blind war veteran in *Scent of a Woman* (1992).

If Steven Bauer's post-*Scarface* career has only been punctuated by only a handful of major movies, including the underrated *Thief of Hearts* (1984), Brian De Palma's *Raising Cain* (1992), *Primal Fear* (1996), and *Traffic* (2000), he has made up in quantity what his filmography lacks in quality. The hard-working actor has become a regular fixture of B-movies such as *Snapdragon* (1993), *The Versace Murder* (1998), and *Raptor Island* (2004), often appearing in anything up to half a dozen movies every year.

Just two years after *Scarface*, Robert Loggia appeared in what has proven to be his most memorable role, as the foul-mouthed but gentle-natured private investigator Sam Ransom in the hit romantic thriller *Jagged Edge* (1985). The role won him an Academy Award nomination as Best Actor in a Supporting Role. Even well into his seventies, the actor continues with a hectic roster of film roles that would exhaust an actor a third of his age. High points of his career include appearances as a vampire mobster in the cult favorite *Innocent Blood* (1992), the sci-fi blockbuster *Independence Day* (1996) and David Lynch's *Lost Highway* (1997).

Like Loggia, F Murray Abraham didn't have long to wait for recognition by the Academy of Motion Picture Arts and Sciences. While he was busy shooting *Scarface*, he was approached by the Czech director Milos Forman to star as the spiteful composer Antonio Salieri in the 1994 film version of Peter Shaffer's stage play *Amadeus*. Forman had decided that he wanted to make a clean break from the original 1980 Broadway production and didn't want Ian McKellen to recreate on film the role he had inaugurated in the London, Washington and New York runs of the play. Abraham won the Oscar for Best Actor for his performance and, thereafter, became a character actor in almost constant demand around the world.

It is ironic, given the generally thankless nature of their roles in the movie, that the two people who probably benefited most from *Scarface* were Michelle Pfeiffer and Mary Elizabeth Mastrantonio. Pre-*Scarface*, both were virtual unknowns struggling to make it in the acting business; post-*Scarface*, both had their pick of roles from the cream of prospective screenplays. Mastrantonio went on to star in Martin Scorsese's *The Color of Money* (1986), James Cameron's *The Abyss* (1989), and opposite Kevin Costner in the blockbuster hit *Robin Hood: Prince of Thieves* (1991). Pfeiffer had three Oscar nominations in her future and has become one of the highest-paid, most highly respected and most popular actresses in Hollywood, thanks to successful movies such as *Married to the Mob* (1988), *Dangerous Liaisons* (1988), *The Fabulous Baker Boys* (1989), *Batman Returns* (1992), *The Age of Innocence* (1993), *One Fine Day* (1996), and *What Lies Beneath* (2000).

Just about everyone involved with *Scarface* has flourished to a greater or lesser extent, putting paid to the old cliché that crime doesn't pay.

When *Scarface* vanished from theaters, it didn't disappear into obscurity as so many films had done in the past. The film benefited from a revolution in electronics that transformed the way films were delivered to an audience: the home video cassette recorder.

The technology to record images and sound onto magnetic tape had existed since the mid-1950s, but it was only ten years later that the notion of a home-based system for recording television signals became a reality and a further decade before the first compact, affordable VCRs came on the market. Initially, Hollywood lobbied heavily against the VCR. The MPAA's Jack Valenti even addressed the US Congress on the matter, demanding the equipment be banned on the grounds that it encouraged piracy. The fight was taken all the way to the Supreme Court, where it was eventually defeated.

What Hollywood was later to realize, of course, was that whilst VCRs undoubtedly did create an environment for distributing bootleg copies of movies, this was far outstripped by their value as a medium for marketing legitimate copies of their product. The 1980s saw an explosion of VCRs making their ways into people's homes and a high demand for movies to be viewed on this new equipment. The concept of being able to watch any film in the comfort of your own armchair just a matter of months after it had been released at the cinema was irresistible.

Thus even a film such as *Scarface*, which had underperformed at the box office, had an indefinite shelf life on video. It reinforced the whole notion of a 'sleeper' movie: a film underappreciated at the time of its initial release which later developed a cult following. There were any number of films of the 1980s that had enjoyed only a modest success at the cinema—films such as *The Terminator* (1984) and *Streets of Fire* (1984)—that only found their true audience on video.

Scarface was a film that improved on multiple viewings, which would have been prohibitively expensive at the cinema. Its devotees wanted to be able to replay their favorite scenes again and again, chanting Oliver Stone's memorable dialog along with the characters. It was, in many ways, a far more meaningful experience on video than it had been on the big screen. It was a film *about* the 1980s and thus was best experienced through the visual medium of choice of the 1980s.

23

"Every dog has his day."

Tony Montana

Martin Bregman maintains that *Scarface* was a cult movie from the day it was released.

"It started right from the beginning," Bregman affirms. "An audience was developed by the film right at the very beginning: college kids, inner city kids, musicians."

The film spoke to youths living in inner city ghettoes, who didn't see Tony Montana as a stone killer or, to use the words of Omar Suarez in the movie, "a fucking peasant." To them he was a poor immigrant who had pulled himself up the only way he could. He had come to America with nothing and had amassed everything: the money, the cars, the property, the women, the respect. All on his own terms.

They sympathized with him. They identified with him. His struggle was their struggle.

"Tony Montana was a product of his time," Bregman explained. "He came to this country not to blow up banks, not to go into the cocaine business, but this is what was available to him. As many, many poor people find when they come to the States and there's nothing open for them. Someone like Tony Montana, who had a bit of a criminal background, didn't know where to go. So, like many others, he fell within this criminal groove. But he was an heroic figure, he was a man that had integrity, he was a man that climbed very quickly based on his intelligence and his toughness, to become a king of industry. His industry just happened to be cocaine."

Hardly surprisingly, *Scarface* became a touchstone in the rise of gangsta rap. Houston hip-hop star and music mogul Brad Jordan adopted the stage name Scarface when he was part of the Geto Boys and the band recorded a song in honor of the movie, sampling snatches of dialog from the soundtrack. After going solo, Jordan released a 1995 album entitled *The World is Yours*. "I took on the Scarface name because that was me, man," he said.

Ray 'Benzino' Scott of *The Source* magazine explained: "If you was a comic book lover, you loved *Batman*. If you was out on the streets, you loved *Scarface*." Rapper Fat Joe went further, describing Tony Montana was "the ultimate ghetto superhero."

Sean Combs, the superstar record producer and music mogul known variously as Puff Daddy and P Diddy, reckons to have watched *Scarface* more than 50 times. "I'd say the movie was the most culturally impactful for our generation, because our generation was really put here with nothing. Statistically, being young and black and coming up in the 1980s you were either gonna end up dead or in jail. Tony Montana was like a lot of us: backed up against a wall. He had to fight to try to make it in this world. That's one of the reasons why minorities relate to it so much. Especially black, inner city minorities. Drug dealing and drug selling were the only way we saw an out."

As Combs sees it, Tony Montana was part anti-hero and part role model. "He was an upstanding gangsta, which is rare. He played by rules and morals." His downfall also served as a cautionary tale about overreaching oneself. "I think I was definitely one of the cats that was scared straight by the movie," Combs laughs. "Me being an extremist, I knew that I would have ended up just like Scarface."

The extent to which *Scarface* had achieved iconic status with the hip-hop community can be measured by the fact that, when the film was re-released in theaters in 2003, Universal Pictures suggested to Bregman and De Palma that they wipe Giorgio Moroder's music from the soundtrack and rescore the film with rap music. It's also more than likely that Universal had their eye on being able to release a lucrative soundtrack album featuring whatever new music was selected for use in the film.

Having seen the way that acceptance of the film had grown in the intervening years, De Palma was vehemently opposed to the gimmicky notion of crassly bolting on an up-to-the minute musical score. "They said it would help promotion, presenting the film in a different way," he explained. "But Giorgio's music was true to the period, I argued. No one changes the scores on movies by Martin Scorsese, John Ford, David Lean. If this is the masterpiece you say it is, then leave it alone. I fought them tooth and nail, and was the odd man out—not an unusual place for me. I have final cut, so that stopped them dead."

The film was re-released with its original score intact.

If *Scarface* spoke to the Have-nots of the world, Oliver Stone also believes it spoke directly to the Haves. Intentionally or not, he seemed to have tapped into the zeitgeist of Ronald Reagan's America.

"I go on the New York subway and I hear dialog from the movie," Stone said. "A lot of young lawyers and businessmen quote me the dialog, and I say 'Why do you remember this?' They say 'It's exactly like my business.' Apparently, the gangster ethics hit on some of the business ethics going on in this country."

Stone has also found the film has served as his calling card. "*Scarface* has probably got me more free champagne everywhere in the world than any film I've ever worked on. Gangsters I've bumped into in Paris—gay gangsters—bought me champagne and said 'How did you *know?*' When I went to El Salvador, I got a lot of my 'ins' with Major D'Aubisson and the right-wing Arena Party because they loved *Scarface*. I was the man who wrote it. I was *muy macho*."

Martin Bregman has noted how the critics have slowly changed their tune about the film. "The critics hated the film initially. The critics didn't understand what we were doing. There wasn't a major reviewer in this country, with the exception of Vincent Canby in the *New York Times*, who thought this wasn't garbage. Now these same reviewers have pointed to *Scarface* as the consummate gangster film, as the landmark gangster film."

Similarly, Hollywood bigwigs have gradually revised their opinion of the film. Brian De Palma was probably only half kidding when he observed: "This community loathed *Scarface* because the characters were so much like them. Manipulative. Loathsome."

But Hollywood has always been the most fickle town on the planet and, once the initial furore had died down and the film began establishing genuine cult status, industry figures fell over themselves to change their tune.

Marty Bauer, Brian De Palma's agent, has this to say of his former colleagues at the William Morris talent agency: "*Scarface* was a movie that some of my colleagues at William Morris wouldn't go to the party afterward... As time has gone by, *Scarface* is now considered a good movie. It wasn't then. It was reviled. *Reviled*. Now they think it's a great movie. They watch it over and over on their videocassettes. Up in their trillion-dollar homes they're all watching it and loving every second of it. When it came out they hated it."

Similarly, De Palma himself has observed that Al Pacino's performance in *Scarface* has attained an almost legendary status within the acting profession. "Every actor I've ever met does Tony Montana. Bruce Willis does an incredible Tony Montana. Or Tom Cruise. Or Alec Baldwin. They all do him. It's like we used to do Marlon Brando in *On the Waterfront*. It's such an audacious character, with such wonderful lines, and Al did such an incredible performance that every actor in the world loves to play that part."

Scarface has also been paid tribute by numerous other films. It has been referenced in *Lock, Stock and Two Smoking Barrels* (1998), *New Jack City* (1991), *Never Die Alone* (2004), *L'Appat* (1995), *The Real McCoy* (1993), *Paid in Full* (2002), *The Master of Disguise* (2002), *Meet the Fockers* (2004), and just about every gangster comedy of the last twenty years. The animated comedy *Shark Tale* (2004) turned Tony Montana into a vengeful shrimp. In *Rush Hour 2* (2001), the palm-tree mural on the wall of the "Paradise On Earth" massage parlor is a copy of the mural in Frank Lopez's office. Oliver Stone included a clip from the film in *Natural Born Killers* (1994), with Mickey (Woody Harrelson) watching *Scarface* on television and commenting, "Why they make all these fuckin' stupid movies? Don't they believe in kissin' anymore? I tell ya, out there in Hollywood, somebody's a taco short of a combo plate." Even the bestselling computer game *Grand Theft Auto: Vice City* features a replica of Tony Montana's office in his Coral Gables mansion.

And in a recent poll, *Maxim* magazine voted Tony Montana as the Biggest Movie Badass of All Time.

Over the course of more than two decades since its theatrical release, *Scarface* has become absorbed into popular culture.

For Brian De Palma, time has validated the choices he made back in the early 1980s.

"You have to pay less attention to what's being said about you when the movie comes out. When a movie's released, you're always measured against the fashion of the times. And the work goes on. In retrospect, all you want is your work to be around, maybe a couple of decades, maybe into the next century if it's *really* good.

"We got our heads handed to us at the time. The movie scandalized everybody. But, in retrospect, you say 'This was *really* good.'"

fade out...

"Say good night to the bad guy."

Tony Montana

Brian De Palma, Martin Bregman and Al Pacino joined forces again in 1993 for *Carlito's Way*, the tale of an Hispanic gang leader who emerges from prison determined to go straight, but who finds it impossible to leave behind his life of crime. If one is feeling speculative, one might think of the film as being the sequel to *Scarface* that never was. Carlito Brigante is who Tony Montana might have become, ten years clean, had he not been gunned down in the fountain at Coral Gables. Or maybe it was just another cool gangster flick.

Brian De Palma eventually forgave Oliver Stone for his ill-advised letter critiquing *Scarface*. In 1987, in response to a question by the author as to the fate of his pet project, *The Demolished Man*, the director confided that he and Stone had collaborated on yet another version of the screenplay but that it was languishing somewhere at home. "Maybe I ought to go take another look at it," he said wistfully. We're still waiting, Brian.

Brian De Palma stopped referring to Michelle Pfeiffer as "that Pink disaster". In 1990, he invited her to appear as Maria Ruskin, the mistress of "master of the universe" Sherman McCoy, in his adaptation of Tom Wolfe's novel *The Bonfire of the Vanities*, but Pfeiffer was involved in making *The Russia House* and declined the offer. Instead, Melanie Griffith, one time wife of Steven Bauer, took the role. In the end, both *The Bonfire of the Vanities* and *The Russia House* tanked.

Al Pacino finally looked Michelle Pfeiffer in the eye when they were cast as fumbling lovers in the romantic comedy drama *Frankie and Johnny* in 1991. She said, "I warned him that I was going to tell people that he had become much nicer, and I had become much meaner." He said, "Maybe I was just a jerk and I didn't know it. It always happens that way."

And...

In the winter of 2004, there was an announcement in the Hollywood trade press regarding yet another version of *Scarface*. This would be a *Scarface* for the new millennium: a four-hour TV mini-series with an all-black cast and set in Los Angeles, which would catapult the story into the modern world of gangstas and crack-cocaine houses.

You just can't keep a bad guy down.

appendix 1

Scarface Credits (*1932 Version*)

Cast:
Tony Camonte: Paul Muni
Cesca Camonte: Ann Dvorak
Guino Rinaldo: George Raft
Johnny Lovo: Osgood Perkins
Tom Gaffney: Boris Karloff
Poppy: Karen Morley
Ben Guarino: C Henry Gordon
Chief of Detectives: Edwin Maxwell
Angelo: Vince Barnett
Mama Camonte: Inez Palange
Louis Costillo: Harry J Vejar
Pietro: Henry Armetta
Epstein: Bert Starkey
MacArthur: John Lee Mahin
Mr Garston: Purnell Pratt
Managing Editor: Tully Marshall
Reporter: Eddie Fetherston
Mabel: Virginia Dabney
Sadie Thompson: Helen C Thompson
Jim: Maurice Black
Janitor: Hank Mann
Waiter: Gino Corrado
Orchestra Leader: Gustav Arnheim

Dancer: Warner P Richmond
Dancer: Dennis O'Keefe
Citizens Committee Member: Eugenie Besserer
Citizens Committee Member: William B Davidson
Citizens Committee Member: Brandon Hurst
Hood: Paul Fix
Hood: John Kelly
Hood: Jack Terry
Hood: Charles Sullivan
Hood: Harry Tenbrook
Meehan: Howard Hawks

Crew:
Director: Howard Hawks
Producers: Howard Hughes/Howard Hawks
Screenplay: Ben Hecht/Seton I Miller/John Lee Mahin/WR Burnett/Fred Pasley
Directors of Photography: Lee Garmes/L William O'Connell
Editor: Edward Curtiss (supervised by Douglas Biggs)
Art Director: Harry Oliver
Music: Adolph Tandler/Gustav Arnheim
Assistant Director: Richard Rosson
Sound: William Snyder
Production Manager: Charles Stallings
Camera Operators: Roy Clark/Warren Lynch
Camera Assistants: Charles Bohny/Warner Cruze

appendix 2

Scarface Credits (*1983 Version*)

Cast:
Antonio 'Tony' Montana: Al Pacino
Manolo 'Manny' Rivera: Steven Bauer
Elvira Hancock: Michelle Pfeiffer
Gina Montana: Mary Elizabeth Mastrantonio
Frank Lopez: Robert Loggia
Omar Suarez: F Murray Abraham
Alejandro Sosa: Paul Shenar
Mel Bernstein: Harris Yulin
Mama Montana: Miriam Colon
Alberto the Shadow: Mark Margolis
Nick the Pig: Michael P Moran
Hector the Toad: Al Israel
Chi Chi: Angel Salazar
Ronnie Echevierra: John Contardo
Miguel Echevierra: John Contardo
Orlando Gutierrez: Carlos Cestero
Ernie: Arnaldo Santana
Angel Fernandez: Pepe Serna
Emilio Rebenga: Roberto Contreras
George Sheffield: Michael Alldredge
Seidelbaum: Ted Beniades
Luis: Paul Espel
Dr Munoz: Loren Almaguer

Miriam: Dawnell Bowers
Pedro Quinn: Albert Carrier
Vic Phillips: John Carter
General Eduardo Strasser: Dante D'André
Charles Goodson: Gregg Henry (uncredited)
Ariel Bleyer: Victor Millan
Nacho 'El Gordo' Contreras: Joe Marmo
Gaspar Gomez: Robert Van Den Berg
Fernando: Richard Delmonte
Waldo: Santos Morales
Mrs Gutierrez: Ilka Payan
Gutierrez Child 1: Angela Nisi
Gutierrez Child 2: Heather Benna
Marta: Barbra Perez
The Skull: Geno Silva
Octavio the Clown: Wayne Doba
MC at Babylon Club: Richard Belzer
Banker: Dennis Holahan
Bank Spokesman: John McCann
Interviewer: Mario Machado
Nacho's Bodyguard: Ray Martel
Gaspar's Bodyguard: Mike Moroff
Gina's Killer: Richard Mendez
Monsignor: Michael Rougas
Immigration Officers: Garnett Smith, Tony Perez,
John Brandon
Immigration Officers (voice): Dennis Franz (uncredited)
    Charles Durning (uncredited)
Cuban Refugees: Gil Barreto, Troy Isaacs, Jim Towers
Saleslady: Tina Leigh Cameron

Car Salesman: Ronald Joseph

Marielito: Robert Hammer Cannerday

Shooters: Rene Carrasco, Gary Cervantes, Gregory N Cruz

Drivers: Richard Caselnova, Tony Pann

Cook: Caesar Cordova

Maitre d': Michel Francois

Male Patron: Ben Frommer

Taco Stand Customer: Edward R Frommer

Helicopter Pilots: John Gamble, Chuck Tamburo

Cuban Man: Bob Yanez

Kid: Arnold Tafolla, Manuel Padilla Jr

Women at Babylon Club: Angela Aames, Nancy Lee
   Andrews, Dona Baldwin, Rosa Lee Benton, Cynthia Burr,
   Lana Clarkson, Karen Criswell, Margo Kelly, Ava Lazar,
   Emilia Lesniak, Marii Mak, Shelley Taylor Morgan,
   Catharine Richardson, Pat Simmons, Terri Taylor, Charlie
   Adiano, Lisa Katz, Jeanette Linné, Margaret Michaels,
   Rhonda Sandberg, Kathy Shea, Marcia Wolf

Stunts: Jim Arnett, Bobby Bass, Clay Boss, Janet Brady, Jerry
   Brutsche, Chere Bryson, David Burton, Dave Cadiente,
   Steve Chambers, Gary Combs, Gil Combs, Steve
   Davison, Tim Davison, Mike De Luna, Justin De Rosa,
   Eddy Donno, Tom Elliott, David Ellis, Gary Epper,
   Eurlyne Epper, Lenny Geer, Alan Gibbs, James M Halty,
   Fred Hice, Bill Hooker, Buddy Joe Hooker, Hugh
   Hooker, Thomas J Huff, Gary Hymes, Al Jones, Donna
   Keegan, Ed Lang, Buck McDancer, Gary McLarty, John
   Meier, Alan Oliney, Ron Oliney, Brad Orrison, Chuck
   Picerni Jr, Donald Pulford, JN Roberts, Mario Roberts,
   Sandy Robertson, Thomas Rosales Jr, Mike Runyard,

Sharon Schaffer, Spike Silver, Eddie Smith, Peter T
Stader, Tom Steele, Ron Stein, Keith Tellez, Jack Verbois,
Danny Weselis, Glen Wilder, Scott Wilder, Dick Ziker

Crew:
Director: Brian De Palma
Screenplay: Oliver Stone
Producer: Marin Bregman
Executive Producer: Louis A Stroller
Co-Producer: Peter Saphier
Director of Photography: John A Alonzo
Editors: Jerry Greenberg/David Ray
Art Director: Ed Richardson
Visual Consultant: Ferdinando Scarfiotti
Music: Giorgio Moroder
Casting: Alixe Gordin
Unit Production Manager: Ray Hartwick
First Assistant Directors: Jerry Ziesmer/Joe Napolitano
Second Assistant Director: Chris Soldo
Set Decorator: Bruce Weintraub
Leadman: Dan May
Set Dressers: Will Waters/Casey Hallenbeck
Assistant Art Director: Jim Allen
Set Designers: Blake Russell/Steve Schwartz/Geoff Hubbard
Camera Operators: Michael Ferris/John Toll/Tom
Laughridge
Assistant Camera Operators: Horace Jordan Jr/Mario
    Zavala/Michael Chavez/Susan Ingram
Still Photographer: Sidney Baldwin
Make-Up: Steve Abrums/Barbara Guedel

Hair Stylists: Toni Walker/Janice Brandow
Property Master: John Zemansky
Assistant Property Masters: Bob Widin/Ed Villa
Location Managers: Frank Pierson/Susan Zwerman
Key Grip: Bud Heller
Dolly Grip: Clyde Smith
Best Boy Grip: Don Glenn
Grip: Don Schmitz
Gaffer: Stuart Spohn
Best Boys: Dutch Presley/Bob Mundell
Electricians: Michael Barrett/Kevin Presley
Special Effects: Ken Pepiot/Stan Parks
Construction Coordinator: Lynn Price
Carpenter Foremen: Pete Ivy/Peter Lamppu/Carlos Salinas
Stunt Coordinator: Jophery Brown
Production Coordinator: Shari Leibowitz
Script Supervisor: Jan Kemper
Costume Designer: Patricia Norris
Costumers: Tony Scarano/Linda Henrikson/Greg Pena
Unit Publicist: Joan Eisenberg
Additional Casting: Bob Morones
Extra Casting: Karl Brindle/Billy Cardenas
Talent Coordinator: Judee Roberts
Craft Service: Joe James
DGA Trainee: Bob Yanetti
Production Assistants: Michael Fottrell/Darryl Fong/Lori Meeks
Sound Mixer: Charles Darin Knight
Boom Operator: Don Bolger
Recordist: Charles Bond
Re-recording Mixer: Buzz Knudsen

Sound Effects Recordist: Andy Aaron
Transportation Coordinator: Danny Anglin
Transportation Captain: Ted Reed
Transportation Co-captain: Bob Cornnell
Drivers: Richard Brehm/Junior Newman/Pat Seran/Frankie
    Hernandez/Tony Emerzian
2nd Unit Director & Title Sequence Design:
    David Hans Dreyfuss
Title Sequence Editor: Paul Neshamkin
Additional 2nd Assistant Director: James Herbert
Associate Film Editor: Bill Pankow
Assistant Film Editors: Ray Hubley/Laura Civiello/
    David Oakden
Supervising Sound Editor: Edward Beyer
Sound Editors: Maurice Schell/Paul Trejo/Michael Jacobi/Lou
    Graf/Kevin Lee/Mark Rathaus/Michael Kirchberger/
    Jay Dranch/Robert H Cornett
Looping Dialogue Editors: Harriet Fidlow/Hal Levinsohn
Music Editor: Jim Henrikson
Assistant Sound Editors: Leslie Troy Gaulin/Bruce
    Kitzmeyer/Joan Metzger/Wendie Phifer-Mate/
    Weezie Rubacky/Annie Stein/Barbara Minor/
    Yvette Nabel/Marissa DeGuzman/Arthur Weiss/Brunilda
    Torres/Randall Coleman/Maddy Shirazi/James Briley
Editing Room Assistants: Michael Bregman/Alfred Laurence
    Kahn/Debby Paley/Shari Smith/Robert Yano/Lori
    Kornspun
Music Editor: Jim Henrikson
Music Arrangers: Arthur Barrow/Sylvester Levay/Giorgio
    Moroder/Kristian Schultze/Richie Zito

Music Co-ordinator: Laurie Kanner
Technical Sound Consultant: David Concors
Sound Consultants: Steve Hodge/Brian Reeves/David Rideau
Video Consultant: Hal Landeker
Technicolor Consultant: Phil Hetos
Technicolor Timing Consultant: Jack Garsha
Rear Projection: Bill Hansard
Negative Cutter: Donah Bassett
Titles & Optical Effects: Computer Opticals
Publicity: Zarem Inc
Dialogue Coach: Robert Easton
Assistant to Mr De Palma: Gary Hill
Assistant to Mr Pacino: Mary Viviano
Secretaries: Barbrah Messing/Sandy Russell
Production Auditors: Ron Filbert/Willie Kapahu
Catering: Michaelson's

Music:
Scarface (Push it to the Limit)
Music: Giorgio Moroder
Lyrics: Pete Bellotte
Performed by Paul Engemann

Rush Rush
Music: Giorgio Moroder
Lyrics: Deborah Harry
Performed by Deborah Harry

Turn Out the Light
Music: Giorgio Moroder
Lyrics: Pete Bellotte
Performed by Amy Holland

Vamos a Bailar
Music: Giorgio Moroder
Lyrics: Maria Conchita
Performed by Maria Conchita

She's On Fire
Music: Giorgio Moroder
Lyrics: Pete Bellotte
Performed by Amy Holland

Shake It Up
Music: Giorgio Moroder
Lyrics: Giorgio Moroder/Arthur Barrow
Performed by Elizabeth Daily

Dance Dance Dance
Music: Giorgio Moroder
Lyrics: Giorgio Moroder/Arthur Barrow
Performed by Beth Andersen

I'm Hot Tonight
Music: Giorgio Moroder
Lyrics: Giorgio Moroder/Arthur Barrow
Performed by Elizabeth Daily

Tony's Theme
Music: Giorgio Moroder
Performed by Giorgio Moroder

Gina's and Elvira's Theme
Music: Giorgio Moroder
Performed by Giorgio Moroder

Strangers in the Night
Music: Bert Kaempfert
Lyrics: Charles Singleton/Eddie Snyder

Music Coordinator: Amy Ross

The Producers would like to give special thanks to:
The Organized Crime Bureau of Broward County, especially
Major Nick Novarro and Agent Rafael Hernandez Jr
The Goodyear Tire & Rubber Company and crew of the
Enterprise

Documentary Footage of the Cuban Boat People
furnished by:
National Broadcasting Company Inc
Sherman Grinberg Film Libraries Inc
Seven League Productions Inc
Tri-Continental Film Center Foundation
Wometco Enterprises Inc

Filmed in Panavision
Color by Technicolor

appendix 3

Richard Belzer, who plays the MC at the Babylon Club was an actual stand-up comedian at the time the movie was made. He later became a household name as Detective John Munch in the television series *Homicide: Life on the Streets* and *Law & Order*.

Octavio, the clown performing at the Babylon Club, was played by mime artist Wayne Doba. Doba also appeared as the monster in Tobe Hooper's horror film *The Funhouse* (1981).

Actress Lana Clarkson, who appears as an extra in the Babylon Club, was found shot dead in the home of record producer Phil Spector on February 3, 2003. Spector was subsequently indicted for her murder.

Tony and Manny's first official job in Miami is slaving at the El Paraiso food stand. As an in-joke, the name El Paraiso was later used as the name of the nightclub in the subsequent Brian De Palma/Martin Bregman/Al Pacino gangster collaboration *Carlito's Way* (1993).

Singer Maria Conchita, who performs the song *Vamos a Bailar* on the Scarface soundtrack, is better known as actress Maria Conchita Alonso and has appeared in movies such as *The Running Man* (1987), *Extreme Prejudice*

(1987), *Colors* (1988), *Predator 2* (1990) and *The House of the Spirits* (1993).

Singer Elizabeth Daily, who performs the songs *Shake It Up* and *I'm Hot Tonight* on the *Scarface* soundtrack, has also appeared in the cult movies *Streets of Fire* (1984) and *Pee-Wee's Big Adventure* (1985). However, she is better known as EG Daily, who has supplied the voices of Tommy Pickles in *Rugrats*, Buttercup in *The Powerpuff Girls* and Babe in *Babe: Pig in the City* (1998).

During the infamous chainsaw sequence, the film playing on the television in Hector the Toad's hotel room is *Earthquake* (1974).

Miami-born Brett Ratner, director of such films as *Rush Hour* (1998), *Red Dragon* (2002) and *After the Sunset* (2004), claims to have been one of the children hired as extras during the scene where Tony and Manny walk past a crowded swimming pool.

It has long been rumored that the band Blink-182 took the numerical aspect of their name from the number of times the word "fuck" is uttered in *Scarface*. Notwithstanding the fact that the profanity appears in excess of 200 times during the movie, band member Mark Hoppus has also confirmed "It doesn't mean anything, we just pulled it out of our ass."

In 2003, an author working under the pseudonym Dejohn self-published an unofficial sequel to *Scarface* entitled *The Return of SF*. Dejohn claimed to be a writer and philosopher who had spent 20 years working in law enforcement.

selected bibliography

Books

Base, Ron, *"If the Other Guy Isn't Jack Nicholson, I've Got the Part": Hollywood Tales of Big Breaks, Bad Luck and Box-Office Magic*, Contemporary Books, Chicago, 1994

Biskind, Peter, *Easy Riders, Raging Bulls*, Simon and Schuster, New York, 1998

Bouzereau, Laurent, *The De Palma Cut*, Dembner Books, New York, 1988

Bouzereau, Laurent, *The Cutting Room Floor*, Citadel Press, New York, 1994

Dworkin, Susan, *Double De Palma: A Film Study with Brian De Palma*, Newmarket Press, New York, 1984

King, Stephen, *On Writing*, Scribner, New York, 2000

Knapp, Laurence F. (Editor), *Brian De Palma: Interviews*, University Press of Mississippi, Jackson, 2003

Larson, Erik, *The Devil in the White City*, Vintage, New York, 2004

McBride, Joseph, *Hawks on Hawks*, University of California Press, Los Angeles, 1982

Miller, Frank, *Censored Hollywood: Sex, Sin & Violence on Screen*, Turner Publishing, Atlanta, 1994

O'Brien, Geoffrey, *Hardboiled America: The Lurid Years of Paperbacks*, Van Nostrand Reinhold, New York, 1981

Pollock, Dale, *Skywalking: The Life and Films of George Lucas*, Ballantine Books, New York, 1983

Salamon, Julie, *The Devil's Candy: The Bonfire of the Vanities Goes to Hollywood*, Delta Books, New York, 1992

Silet, Charles L. P. (Editor), *Oliver Stone: Interviews*, University Press of Mississippi, Jackson, 2001

Thompson, Douglas, *Pfeiffer: Beyond The Age of Innocence*, Warner Books, London, 1995

Trail, Armitage, *Scarface*, Bloomsbury, London, 1997

Periodicals

"The Sound and *The Fury*", *Films Illustrated*, December 1979
"Half Hitch", *The Guardian*, December 1980
"An Interview with the Kings of Horror", *Oui*, August 1981
"20 Questions: Brian De Palma", *Playboy*, December 1983
"Gunning Their Way to Glory", *Newsweek*, December 1983
"Pacino's Way", *The Guardian*, December 2004

Miscellaneous

Scarface (1932) (CIC Video, 1986)
Scarface (1983) (CIC Video, 1987)
Scarface (1983), *Two-Disc Anniversary Edition* DVD (Universal Pictures (UK) Ltd, 2003)
Scarface, Screenplay by Oliver Stone
Scarface, Production Notes (United International Pictures)
http://www.briandepalma.net
http://www.crimelibrary.com

index

Abraham. F. Murray 126, 145, 196–7

Alda, Alan 9, 195

All the President's Men (1976) 80

Allen, Nancy 69, 75, 77, 79–80, 82, 131

Alonzo, John A. 135–6, 142, 145–6, 147, 148–9, 154, 165

American Gigolo (1980) 146, 165

American Graffiti (1973) 66

American International Pictures 79

Ansen, David 186

Apocalypse Now (1979) 105, 123

Atkins, Dr Richard 180

Barnett, Vince 46

Bauer, Marty 124, 205

Bauer, Steven 124–5, 131, 144, 185, 193, 196

BBFC (British Board of Film Classification) 180–3

Bergen, Candice 9

Berkley Publishing Group 166

Bester, Alfred 68

Big Sleep, The (1946) 30

Biskind, Peter 61

Blow Out (1981) 78–83, 85

Blue Ice (1992) 195

Body Double (1984) 193–4

Bone Collector, The (1999) 195

Bonfire of the Vanities, The (1990) 194

Born on the Fourth of July (1989) 105–6, 195

Brandel, Marc 109

Brecht, Bertolt 11

Bregman, Martin 9–12, 57, 83, 96, 105, 112, 118, 119, 122, 124–5, 128–9, 139–41, 162, 170–2, 177–8, 179–80, 195, 201–2, 204, 209

Bringing Up Baby (1938) 30

British Board of Film Classification (BBFC) 180–3

Brynner, Yul 62

Buñuel, Luis 59, 77

Cain, James M. 24

Caine, Michael 110

"Call Me" 164

Calley, John 61

Canby, Vincent 186, 204

Capone, Al 15–20, 23, 34–6, 38, 51, 88

Capone (1973) 10

CARA (Classification and Ratings Administration) 175–80

Carlito's Way (1993) 209

Carrie (1976) 67–8, 78

Carter, President Jimmy 92–5

Castro, Fidel 92–5, 119

Cat People (1982) 146

"Cat People (Putting Out Fire)" 165

Chandler, Raymond 24

Chaplin, Charlie 144

Churchill, Winston 144

Classification and Ratings Administration (CARA) 175–80

Clayburgh, Jill 59

Cleopatra (1963) 32
Clockwork Orange, A (1971) 176
Cocks, Jay 180
Colosimo, "Big Jim" 36
Columbia Pictures 105, 106, 193
Combs, Sean 202–3
Come and Get It (1936) 30
Conan the Barbarian (1982) 109
Conformist, The (1970) 146
Contreras, Roberto 143
Coons, Maurice 21, 23, 36, 44, 49–50
Coppola, Francis Ford 10, 58, 66, 82, 105, 123, 140
Coughlin, Mae 18, 20
Cox, Courteney 86
Cox, Elizabeth 111
Crittenden, Jordan 61
Crowd Roars, The (1932) 46
Cruise, Tom 106, 194

Daily Telegraph, The 185
"Dancing in the Dark" 86
Davenport, Mary 73
Dawn Patrol, The (1930) 29
De Niro, Robert 59, 60, 88
De Palma, Brian 57–90, 120–8, 131–2, 136, 139–40, 145–9, 151–64, 168–72, 176–89, 193–4, 203, 204–6, 209
Demolished Man, The (1953) 68, 71
Denby, David 76
Devil's Advocate (1997) 195
Dickinson, Angie 75, 77–8, 160, 193
Dillinger (1973) 10

Dionysus in 69 (1970) 60
Dog Day Afternoon (1975) 10, 57, 91
Donaggio, Pino 164
Douglas, Kirk 70, 73
Dressed to Kill (1980) 59, 75–8, 82, 85, 160
Dreyfuss, Richards 79
Dvorak, Ann 46

Easton, Robert 134
Eastwood, Clint 191
Easy Rider (1969) 60, 164
Einstein, Albert 144
El Dorado (1966) 30
Engemann, Paul 166

Fairbanks, Douglas 30
Farris, John 70
Feinberg, Dr H. 180
Femme Fatale (2002) 194
Ferman, James 181, 182
Filmways Pictures 78–9, 81–2
Finley, William 59, 62, 64
First National Pictures 41
Five Point Youths 16
Flash Gordon (1980) 146
Flashdance (1983) 89, 165
Frankenstein (1931) 46
Frid, Jonathan 108
Friedkin, William 73, 75
Front Page, The (1931) 31
Fury, The (1978) 70, 78

Gallucio, Frank 15, 17
Gentlemen Prefer Blondes (1953) 30
Gere, Richard 71
Get To Know Your Rabbit (1972) 60–1, 62

Giancana, Sam 51–2
Gigli (2003) 195
Gilda (1946) 32
Gillespie, J. Waldron 144
Glengarry Glen Ross (1992) 195
Godard, Jean-Luc 59
Godfather, The (1972) 9, 10, 66, 133, 140
Gone With the Wind (1939) 32
Goodhue, Bertram 144
Gordon, C. Henry 46
Gordon, Keith 71–2, 75–6
Graham, Gerrit 73
Grand Theft Auto: Vice City 206
Grease (1978) 71, 164
Greenberg, Gerald B. 163
Greetings (1968) 59–60, 176
Griffith, Melanie 193, 209
Guys and Dolls (1955) 32

Hammett, Dashiel 23
Hand, The (1981) 109–10
Harrelson, Woody 206
Hatari! (1962) 30
Hawks, Howard 11, 29–31, 36, 38–9, 40–1, 43, 44, 45, 46, 47–9, 51–3, 117
Hays, Postmaster General Will 37, 48, 49
Heat (1995) 195–6
Hecht, Ben 31–3, 34, 35–6, 38–9, 40–1, 48, 116, 117
Heffner, Richard 177, 179
Hell's Angels (1930) 29
Henry, Gregg 153, 193
Hermann, Bernard 63, 65, 164
Hi Mom! (1970) 60

Hill, Walter 61
His Girl Friday (1940) 30
Hitchcock, Alfred 59, 65, 75, 76, 193
Hodges, Mike 146
Holmes, Henry 17
Home Movies (1979) 72–3
Hooper, Tobe 161
Howard, Robert E. 109
Hughes, Howard 11, 28, 29–30, 38–9, 41, 45–6, 47–9, 57, 85

I Am a Fugitive from a Chain Gang (1932) 43
Insider, The (1999) 196
Ioele, Frankie 17
Irving, Amy 69
Israel, Al 160

Jagged Edge (1985) 196
Jaws (1975) 66
JFK (1991) 195
Joy, Jason S. 48
Just Tell Me What You Want (1980) 91

Kael, Pauline 81, 83, 185
Karloff, Boris 46
Katt, William 69
Kidder, Margot 61, 62
King, Stephen 67

Land of the Pharoahs (1955) 30
Last Tango in Paris (1972) 146, 176
Laurentiis, Dino de 109, 194
Laurie, Piper 69
Lepke (1975) 10

Litto, George 82
Loggia, Robert 125–6, 196
Los Angeles Times 63
Lucas, George 58, 61, 66, 68,
  69, 82
Luciano, Charles "Lucky" 17
Lucky Luciano (1974) 10
Lumet, Sidney 57, 72, 91, 118,
  119
Lyne, Adrian 89

MacArthur, Charles 31
Madden Owney 46
Maltin, Leonard 70
Mamet, David 88
Man with the Golden Arm
  (1955) 32
Mankiewicz, Herman 31
Mann, Thomas 144
Mastrantonio, Mary Elizabeth
  127, 130–1, 197
Matilda (1996) 195
Maxim magazine 206
McBain, Ed 62
Midnight Cowboy (1969) 176
Midnight Express (1978)
  106–7, 139
Midnight Run (1988) 167
Milius, John 61, 109
Minnelli, Liza 9
Mission: Impossible (1996)
  194
Mission to Mars (2000) 194
Mizener, Addison 143
Monash, Paul 68, 69
Monette, Paul 167–8
Morley, Karen 46
Moroder, Giorgio 164–6, 193
Motion Picture Association of
  America (MPAA) 175–80

Motion Picture Producers and
  Distributors of America
  (MPPDA) 36–7, 38–41, 47,
  48
Muni, Paul 9, 12, 43–5, 48,
  133
Murder à la Mod (1968)
  59–60, 86

Natural Born Killers (1994)
  195, 206
Ness, Eliot 19
New York Post 185
New York Times 76, 186, 204
New Yorker, The 81, 185
Newsweek 186
Nixon (1995) 195
Nosferatu the Vampire (1979)
  167
Novarro, Major Nick 180

O'Bannion, Charles Dion 35, 36
Obsession (1976) 65–6
One from the Heart (1982) 123
Orion Pictures 72, 82

Pacino, Al 9–10, 11–12, 57, 73,
  79, 88, 105–6, 118, 120, 22,
  124, 125, 129–30, 133–7,
  152, 155, 156, 159–60, 162,
  169–70, 171, 186, 192, 193,
  195–6, 205, 210
Panic in Needle Park (1971) 9
Parallax View, The (1974) 80
Paramount Pictures 31, 89
Parker, Alan 106, 107
Parks, Stan 148, 155
Pasley, Fred 48
Peeping Tom (1959) 75
Pepiot, Ken 148, 155

Perez Jr, Demetrio 141
Perkins, Osgood 46
Pfeiffer, Michelle 127–30, 187, 195, 197, 209–10
Phantom of Paradise (1974) 64–5
Pickford, Mary 30
Platoon (1986) 105, 106
Pluto Nash (2002) 195
Powell, Michael 75
Predator (1987) 167
Pressman, Edward R. 62, 109
Prince of the City (1981) 71–2, 87, 91
Puff Daddy 202–3
Puttman, David 106
Puzo, Mario 10

Rabe, David 71, 87
Racket, The (1928) 38
Raft, George 46–7
Raising Cain (1992) 194, 196
Recruit, The (2003) 195
Red River (1948) 30
Reed, Rex 185
Rehme, Bob 180
Resistible Rise of Arturo Ui, The 11
Reynolds, Burt 62
Rio Bravo (1959) 30
Rolling Stone magazine 76
Rolling Stones 86
Romero, George A. 176
Rosson, Richard 48, 49

Salt, Jennifer 59, 61, 62
Salvador (1986) 194
San Francisco Examiner 63
Saturday Night Fever (1977) 71, 164

Scarface (1932) 29–53
Scarface (novel) 23–8
Scarfiotti, Ferdinando 146–8, 165
Scent of a Woman (1992) 196
Schrader, Paul 61, 65, 146
Scorsese, Martin 58, 61, 68, 82, 88, 108, 127, 185, 197
Scoundrel, The (1934) 31
Sea of Love (1989) 195
Sergeant York (1940) 30
Serna, Pepe 160
Serpico (1973) 10, 57, 91
Shadow, The (1994) 195
Shaft (1970) 164
Shenar, Paul 126–7
Siegel, Benjamin "Bugsy" 46
Sisters (1973) 62–3, 78
Smothers, Tom 60, 61
Snake Eyes (1998) 194
Song Is Born, A (1948) 30
Source magazine 201–2
South Brooklyn Rippers 16
Spacek, Sissy 69
Spacey, Kevin 9
Spielberg, Steven 58, 61, 66, 69, 82, 156–7
Springsteen, Bruce 86
St Valentine's Day Massacre 35, 53
Stone, Oliver 105–22, 131–2, 139–40, 151, 160–1, 167–8, 171–2, 188, 194–5, 203–4, 209
Story of Louis Pasteur, The (1935) 44
Strangers on a Train (1951) 32
Streisand, Barbra 9
Sullivan, Manny 19
Sunna Corporation 11

Superfly (1971) 164
Sweet Liberty (1986) 195

Take One magazine 79
Talk Radio (1988) 195
Tarantino, Quentin 188
Texas Chain Saw Massacre,
    The (1974) 161
Thanks God It's Friday (1978)
    164
Thing from Another World,
    The (1951) 30
Tiger Shark (1932) 30
Time magazine 63, 180
To Have and Have Not (1944)
    30
Torrio, Johnny 16–17, 18
Trail, Armitage 23
Travolta, John 69, 71, 72, 79,
    81, 85, 124
Twentieth Century (1934) 30
20th Century Fox 64

Underworld (1927) 31
United Artists 62, 68
Universal Pictures 11, 57,
    123–4, 146, 165, 180, 203
Untouchables, The (1987) 194

Valenti, Jack 178
Valiant, The (1929) 43
Variety 185–6
Volstead Act (1919) 18

Walker, Gerald 73
Warner Brothers 41, 60, 61, 62,
    72
WAVAW (Women Against
Violence Against Women) 77
Wedding Party, The (1964) 59,
    85
Welch, Raquel 62
Who, The 86
Williams, John 164
Wiz, The (1978) 91
Women Against Violence
    Against Women (WAVAW)
    77

Yale, Frankie 17
Yulin, Harris 127

Ziker, Richard 145
Zsigmond, Vilmos 65

acknowledgments

I would like to thank: Jane Birch, Graham Curd, Mike Evans, Sarah Ford, Sheena Harvey, Patrick Humphries, David Hyman, Maxim Jakubowski, Rebecca Linsdell, Cathy Lowne, Leon Meyer, Abi Rowsell, Yuko Sakai.